Grammar Success

Success

TEACHER'S GUIDE

3

Raising Writing Standards

Pie Corbett   Rachel Roberts

OXFORD

OXFORD
UNIVERSITY PRESS

Great Clarendon Street, Oxford OX2 6DP

Oxford University Press is a department of the University of Oxford.
It furthers the University's objective of excellence in research, scholarship,
and education by publishing worldwide in

Oxford New York

Auckland Bangkok Buenos Aires Cape Town Chennai
Dar es Salaam Delhi Hong Kong Istanbul Karachi Kolkata
Kuala Lumpur Madrid Melbourne Mexico City Mumbai Nairobi
São Paulo Shanghai Taipei Tokyo Toronto

British Library Cataloguing in Publication Data

Data available

3 5 7 9 10 8 6 4 2

ISBN 0 19 834291 8

Designed and produced by Oxford Designers & Illustrators Ltd
Printed in Great Britain by Athenæum Press Ltd, Gateshead, Tyne-and-Wear

Contents

Introduction

Grammar Success is about teaching children how to use grammar to improve their writing. It provides materials, not only to deepen children's grammatical understanding, but also to refine their grammatical skills and to enable them to apply these to their own writing.

Teaching grammatical skills

The course helps pupils to understand grammar but also to become skilful in these key grammatical areas:

- **Sentence construction** – the ability to construct, vary, and control a variety of sentence structures.
- **Punctuation** – the ability to use punctuation to indicate to the reader how a text should be read.
- **Language effects** – the ability to enhance writing, using words powerfully and effectively, plus handling such effects as *simile*, *metaphor*, and *alliteration*.
- **Cohesion** – the ability to create cohesive links within and between sentences, paragraphs, and texts.

It is worth remembering that when children settle down to write, the task can be quite daunting. A good writer has to handle skilfully such basics as handwriting, spelling, and punctuation, as well as controlling sentences and thinking about what to say. Indeed, many children struggle with writing because they fall at the first post: their minds are taken up by worrying over such basics as 'Where does the full stop go?'. If such basic skills are not reasonably automatic, if children are not confident at handling grammar, then their ability to compose will be held back.

This course is founded upon the proposition that becoming skilful at grammar actually can liberate children as writers. The more adept children are at using these skills in their writing, the more freedom they will have to focus upon the actual act of creative composition. Good writers are skilful at handling the building blocks of language. Ted Hughes knew where to put full stops; he was able to focus upon the act of creation.

Teaching sequences

Grammar Success is built around the National Literacy Framework sentence level objectives, and also supports the programmes of study in the Northern Ireland English Curriculum and those of English Language 5–14. However, where there are gaps in the framework, these have been addressed. Additions and slight alterations have been made in the light of teachers' experience of using the framework in the classroom.

In planning the course, attention has been paid to ensuring that sensible links have been created between sentence and text level objectives. After all, the purpose of the sentence level work is to improve the ability to read and write different texts.

Each unit in *Grammar Success* facilitates the teaching of specific sentence level grammar points through a sequence of three or four sessions. The 'one off' lesson too often fails as children need a chance to revisit and to apply what they have been learning. To address this, each unit leads pupils through these three/four stages of learning, using all elements of the course:

Session 1 Activities that introduce children to a particular sentence level feature through whole class use of an OHT and consolidation in a photocopy master (PCM A).

Session 2 Investigating the use of the feature through reading and focused language work in the pupils' book and follow-up PCM B activity.

Session 3 Applying the feature to improve their written work, through shared and independent writing, based on work in the pupils' book.

Session 4 Developing the feature through extension, revision or editing of the writing begun in Session 3.

While a full range of texts and outcomes are provided in the pupils' book, children will gain greater understanding of the grammar if they are taught the four sessions using all three elements of the course.

How the sessions work

Session 1 Session 1 uses an OHT to introduce the grammatical objective to the children. This part of the session should be lively and interactive. The majority of basic grammar teaching can be accomplished through active whole-class teaching. OHTs have a number of advantages over using a worksheet or working on a board:

- It is easy to check that children are watching and engaged.
- The text can be annotated in response to children's ideas. Different features can be underlined in different colours to draw attention to different aspects of a text.
- The text can be projected onto a whiteboard which can be written upon.

Once time has been spent as a whole class looking at an objective, the class moves into independent activities. These are designed around a PCM (all PCMs are flagged ▣) that provides an activity devised to deepen children's understanding and confirm what they have been taught as a whole class. Many of the PCMs are differentiated to allow for pupils who may struggle or who need an extra challenge. Or they could be used flexibly as a homework resource.

By the end of Session 1, pupils should be in a position to define their understanding of the objective. Definition needs to relate not merely to discussing what the feature is – but should also cover how it is used. Pupils may like to keep a literacy glossary into which definitions and points about writing are written. Class wall charts are useful as a way of providing a reminder.

Session 2 uses the pupils' book, plus the PCMs in the Teacher's Guide.

The pupils' book activities focus upon the grammatical feature in the context of wide-ranging stimulus texts. Pupils are asked comprehension questions on each text before moving into activities that focus upon the grammatical feature in use. Session 2 thus moves children's understanding further on, because it is designed to look at the objective in context.

Movement through the session is quite simple – read the stimulus text and think about what it means. Then revisit the text and look carefully at how it has been written. In this way children are encouraged to read as writers – looking constantly at the structures and grammatical features that writers use to create texts and gain effects. The teacher's notes offer questions to ask and points to make in a whole-class introduction.

This time the independent activities are in the pupils' book. Activity A consists of comprehension questions that dig under the skin of the text, deepening children's understanding. Activity B focuses upon the use of the sentence level feature within the text. It revisits the grammatical feature introduced in Session 1 and considers its use within a text.

The plenary, outlined in the teacher's notes, draws all the children together to reconfirm what is known about the sentence level feature. This process should put the large majority of children in the class in a position to understand the feature and to recognize how writers use it effectively within texts. References outwards to other texts are, of course, useful.

By the end of Session 2, pupils have critically reflected upon the use of the objective through their reading.

Session 3 relates again to the text in the pupils' book, which now becomes a model for children's own writing. The teacher's notes describe in detail how to carry out shared writing, demonstrating how to use the grammatical feature in the process of drafting a new text as part of activity C.

The role of shared writing cannot be underestimated as a key approach to teaching writing. During shared writing a number of different teaching strategies can be brought into play:

1 *Demonstration* – the teacher shows children how to use the feature, talking through the writing, explaining its use as an 'expert writer'. The children's role is to sit and listen carefully. Obviously, the modelling needs to be swift and engaging or children may grow restless. However, if the teacher writes directly onto an OHT this has the advantage of the teacher being able to look at the class at a glance, aiding control and drawing children's attention to the teaching points. The teacher rehearses sentences aloud and constantly rereads, checking the writing.

2 *Whole-class composition* – having demonstrated how to use an objective, the teacher moves onto involving the children in actively writing. Obviously this process has to be lively and engaging, challenging children to refine their contributions. There is a danger of merely accepting the first thought that comes into the children's heads. They should be asked to explain ideas and discuss why one idea might be more effective than another. Building in time for children briefly to discuss ideas in pairs is also useful as a way of involving every pupil.

3 *Supported writing* – using whiteboards or notebooks, children have an attempt at using the feature within one or two sentences. This can be supported by a list of ideas, a writing frame or by pair work. The teacher can then check that children can use the objective in a controlled situation, within a few sentences. Once they are confident, children can move into more extended independent composition.

A photocopiable Reminder Sheet in the Teacher's Guide (flagged |R) provides a summary, defining the grammatical feature and giving guidance on how to use it effectively in writing. This could be adapted or added to by the children in the light of their thoughts. Rudimentary understandings can be refined over time. These sheets might be added to the children's literacy glossary, put onto an OHT as a whole-class reminder, or enlarged and displayed as a poster.

Session 3 moves into pupils writing their own work, drawing on the shared writing experience. As pupils write independently, the teacher may wish to work with a group that struggles or to stretch the top end.

Session 4 extends and develops understanding and allows pupils to work on a piece over time. The writing may be continued in later sessions; alternatively, the teacher may revise or edit a piece of previously written work. The Teacher's Guide specifies whether work to be revised/edited should be class writing from Session 3 or pupils' writing (copied onto OHT). The teacher models and supports this stage of the writing process. The emphasis in Session 4 moves to pupils' contributions (i.e. supported writing). Pupils then transfer this learning to the writing they began in Session 3. The focus of the plenary is generally on evaluating the revision, and the impact the learning has had on pupils' individual writing.

Children should become used to concentrating hard during writing. Just before they start it is helpful to remind them of the particular features they should include. As they move through the units, each feature should be added to their growing repertoire of grammatical skills.

End of year hurdles

One of the difficulties that many teachers face is knowing what children should have achieved by the end of any given year. This is easy enough if you happen to be a Year 6 teacher. However, it is less clear for Year 5 teachers. The grid below provides a clear set of markers to aim for. The list relates directly to the level descriptors, the programmes of study, and the literacy framework.

Many children will achieve more than this – the grid provides a base line. A few will not reach this level. However, the grid lists key aspects that can be used as a focus for teaching, for marking, for monitoring, and for target setting.

Of course, not everything has to be tackled at once. During the course of Year 5, children should become more adept in demonstrating the features described. If children can demonstrate these features frequently in their everyday writing, they will be on target for achieving a confident level 5.

Assessing writing

Guidance on marking and assessing pupils' briefer written responses is built in to each unit in this *Teacher's Guide* through assessment notes and model answers. Page 8 offers an example of a child's response (and a teacher's assessment) to a longer written task in activity C of the pupils' book. The sample is by a Year 5 child who has been working on Unit 9 in the pupils' book.

Sentence construction	Punctuation	Language effects	Cohesion	Purpose and organization
Write complex sentences, selecting and using a wide range of subordinators. Adapt or rearrange sentences in relation to text types, using subordinate clauses to add information, to give reasons and to explain. Select appropriate word order in sentences to create interest and to increase precision, clarity and economy. Write using direct and reported speech.	Demarcate at least three out of four sentences correctly using the Y5 range of punctuation marks. Use punctuation to create effects, e.g. slowing the pace of a sentence. Make more use of commas to separate items in a list, clauses and phrases. Use speech marks, with new lines for new speakers and correct punctuation. Secure apostrophe for omission and possession.	Use well-chosen phrases and vocabulary to engage the reader. Use appropriate grammatical features for different text types. *End of Year 5: Statement of Objectives*	Use a repertoire of causal and logical connectives as well as those that signal time, e.g. *however, therefore, next, meanwhile.* Secure grammatical agreement and coherence to avoid ambiguities and contradiction.	In fiction, suggest insights into character development through describing how characters look, react, talk or behave, rather than by telling the reader; use setting to create and reflect changes in mood; use paragraphs to structure plot, by shifting paragraphs for change of time, scene, action, mood or person. In non-fiction, apply features of non-fiction types for use in other curriculum subjects, e.g. instructional texts for technology; elaborate the basic structures of text types in order to make writing more effective in relation to audience and purpose; adapt writing to be concise and clear, and use an impersonal style. In all writing: interest the reader through, for instance, including the narrator's viewpoint, the use of humour, gaining suspense through delay, or by the use of specific detail; draw writing towards a defined conclusion.

Strengths in writing

Good choice of title – it engages the reader.

Direct appeal engages the reader's interest. Correct use of apostrophe for omission (*here's*).

Good use of adjectives to describe the muffin.

Appropriate introduction.

Correct layout for ingredients.

Use of appropriate vocabulary (*cream*).

Apostrophe for omission has been omitted (*its*).

Use of appropriate vocabulary (*light*, *beat*).

Attempt at a complex sentence with 'so' as subordinator.

Vocabulary choice appropriate.

Good choice of *pop*, *bake*, *place*.

Last two sentences are short and to the point.
The final sentence rounds off well – it echoes the initial question.

Areas for development

Possible use of alliteration to emphasize attractiveness; use *ch / m*.

Would work better as two short sentences – a question and answer.

There's no verb in the sentence. Link it to the previous sentence with a colon or dash.

Replace the ellipsis with a colon to introduce the list.

Check with model texts – would the word *of* be used?

Heat your oven to 190°C would work better as a single, short sentence.

Correct use of apostrophe for omission (*it's*)

Could expand the adjective to a phrase for more precision (*light and fluffy / light and pale yellow*).

Replace *very well* with a more appropriate form (e.g. *for two minutes / until completely blended in.*) Same for *mixed in*.

Sentence break before *leave that*.
Consider replacing *that* with *leave to one side*.)
Leave that could be a sentence alone.

As you like is not needed (the number is given in the ingredients).
Specify that the mixture goes into muffin cases, not the baking tray; possible confusion.

Scrumptious Chocolate Muffins

You want to have a chocolate party well here's something you can add to your list. A beautiful, filling chocolate muffin! This is a cracking recipe!

You will need the following . . . . .

150g of soft margarine
150g of caster sugar
3 eggs
150g of self raising flour
50g of cocoa powder
100g of chocolate chips
10/12 muffin cases

Method

Heat your oven to 190°C, cream the sugar and margarine until its a real mixture and make sure it's light. Add all 3 eggs, flour and cocoa powder and beat very well. Stir in milk and add chocolate chips so they get mixed in, leave that and put as many muffin cases as you like onto a baking tray. Fill ¾ full with your mixture then pop it in your oven and bake for 25 minutes. Place on a cooling tray. Are you tempted ?!

Story openings

The purpose of this unit is for pupils to look at the difference between those words that can be used to modify other words and are not essential to meaning, and those that are. It explores the idea of moving words around within a sentence to gain different emphasis. It considers different ways to open a story.

NLS coverage

Key objective

SL 1 To investigate word order by examining how far the order of words in sentences can be changed:
- which words are essential to meaning
- which words can be deleted without damaging the basic meaning
- which words or groups of words can be moved into a different order

Learned through:

TL Reading comprehension
1 To analyse the features of a good opening and compare a number of story openings

Assessment criteria

SL By the end of this unit, pupils should be able to take out or add in modifying words; understand which words are basic to meaning.

TL Writing composition
Children should be able to write a variety of effective story openings, discussing the intended effect on the reader.

Session 1

You will need OHT 1 and PCM 1A.

Shared reading

1 Display OHT 1 and read through the different story openings as a class. Which do pupils think is the most effective? What makes it effective?

2 Take each opening in turn and discuss the impact on the reader – especially thinking about what it is that might raise a question in the reader's mind or make the reader want to read on. For example, what is the panther going to do? Why is Hagwood 'crowded with menace'?

Sentence level work

1 In pairs, ask the children to categorize each opening. There may be different ways to do this, for example:
- dramatic statement
- exclamation
- looking back to a key event
- straight into the action
- main character makes an error, e.g. tells a lie
- dialogue – question opening
- atmospheric scene setting.

2 Imitate the different openings, copying the basic sentence structure, for example:
- *'Run for it!' yelled Dan.*
- *I will never forget the day I ate a worm.*
- *The boy ran. He knew that he was running for his life.*
- *Cassie knew that stealing was wrong.*
- *'Where do you think you are going at this time of night?' said Dad.*
- *At the edge of town, where the houses met the shore, a dry wind whipped the sand up against the window panes so that the beach was deserted.*

3 Spend some time looking at the first opening. Discuss which words are essential to meaning and which could be omitted. Discuss the choice and effect of the words that have been 'added in' for extra description (*black, clear*). Try reordering the words and discuss the effect, e.g. *Silently, the black panther paused at the clear stream, just beyond the estate* or *Just beyond the estate, at the clear stream, the black panther silently paused.*

Independent activities

Direct pupils to PCM 1A. In the first sentence, the children are asked to underline the words that are necessary to meaning in one colour and those that can be taken out in another colour. The children should reorder sentences 2–4, thinking about the different effect they have created. (Generally speaking, whatever comes first is emphasized.) Finally, sentences 5–9 should be categorized and imitated in the same way as the class has worked on the OHT sentences.

Plenary

Take feedback from the PCM activity, listening critically to ideas. Draw up a list of different ways to start a story – add in other strategies for opening that pupils have picked up from previous teaching.

Session 2

You will need pupils' book 3, Unit 1, pages 8–9, and PCM 1B.

Shared reading

1   Turn to the list of story openings in the pupils' book. Read these through. Discuss which is the *least* effective. Make sure that pupils provide reasons for their opinions, quoting from the text and explaining the impact on the reader.

2   Ask pupils to explain all the possible 'clues' that the openings suggest. For instance, the final opening might provoke the following questions – Who are the men? Are they friends? Why are they sitting on a bench on ice? Is this set in an arctic landscape? What are they waiting for? Will the ice break?

Sentence level work

1   Discuss how one example might be reordered and what the effect might be. For example, *'Humans do hate us, why, Uncle Bart?' said Limpy.*

2   Look at the openings and discuss whether effective writing relies on using lots of words that are not essential to meaning but add colour, such as adjectives and adverbs, or whether good writing uses such words sparingly.

Independent activities

Children complete questions A and B in the pupils' book – categorizing and imitating openings, and then experimenting with reordering the openings. Those who complete the task should do the similar activity on PCM 1B to add further openings.

Plenary

Use the plenary to listen to some of the new openings that have been written. Add categories to the class list, and provide good examples. Make sure that in future these are used by the children in their story writing, and noticed in their reading.

Session 3

You will need blank OHTs, pupils' book 3, Unit 1, pages 8–9, and the Reminder Sheet.

Shared writing

Explain that the task is to write an opening paragraph for a story, based on one of the openings that the children have been working on. Revisit briefly the types of opening in the pupils' book. Ask the children to base their opening on one of the following:

■ a dramatic event
■ an interesting setting
■ an interesting character.

Write together

To demonstrate, take one of the openings and imitate the basic structure. Build upon this, taking note of the points made in the pupils' book:

■ varying sentences
■ varying word order for effect
■ varying openings of sentences
■ rereading to check it sounds good
■ selecting words with care
■ thinking about the reader.

For example: *A boy waited at the end of the road. He was only seven years old and he had already waited for an hour. It felt like a lifetime to his small frame. But he did not feel the cold wind tug at his thin jumper. He sniffed bravely. The bus was late, surely. Yet he had waited two years to see his father. What was another few minutes?*

Independent writing activity

The children should read through the instructions in the pupils' book and then write an opening paragraph. Those who complete this quickly could select another opening for the same treatment. In this way they might build up several ready-made story starters.

Plenary

Listen to several examples. Write some on a blank OHT and show them to the class. Look at the sentence construction, discussing whether a different word order might be more effective. Focus upon the impact of the opening, considering whether word choices are effective or just padding.

Session 4

You will need a section of work you have written, or one written by a pupil, on OHT, and the Reminder Sheet.

Shared writing

Remind pupils of the focus – writing interesting openings, carefully choosing words and thinking about the order of the words in sentences.

Write together

1 Display the text which you will be working on. It is useful if you can use a piece of writing that contains some common 'weakness' that appeared in most of the children's writing. Keep the revision focused. It may be useful to use your own example, e.g.

Joanna tapped her foot impatiently on the pavement. Where on earth was her father? She was 11 years old and ballet had always been important to her. She would be late for the class. A nasty wind came down the nasty road. Joanna moved her coat close to her. Honestly, you would have thought that a grown man could keep time.

2 Pick up on places where the writing might be improved or 'corrected', e.g. try reordering the first sentence by moving *impatiently* to the start of the sentence, strengthen *came* and *moved*, improve *nasty* and avoid the repetition.

Independent writing activity

Pupils work together on their writing, taking turns. They should keep in mind any points that have arisen, e.g. avoiding repetition, using powerful verbs, thinking about shifting the adverb.

Plenary

Discuss changes made to pieces of writing. Hear some read aloud – both the original and the new version. Do pupils feel the revised piece is improved? Discuss a possible format for publication, e.g. on display in the classroom, on the school website, in the class scrapbook. Briefly revisit different ways to open stories and the business of adjusting word order to gain effect.

Assessment

Pupils should be able to:
- use modifying words sparingly but effectively
- control sentence construction effectively
- write an effective opening that draws the reader into the narrative.

Model answers

Pupils' book 3 ◁ A

1, 2 Encourage children to explain preferences in terms of impact on the reader. Some openings will fulfil several functions. Encourage pupils to quote from the text to support views.

Pupils' book 3 ◁ B

3 Answers will vary. Accept those listed on the Reminder Sheet and any variations that are appropriate.

4 When reordering the sentences, pupils may need to make a few alterations, changing words or using extra connectives.

◁ 1A Story openings ▣

In the main, the words that are not needed will be adjectives, adverbs, and some extra phrases or subordinate clauses, e.g. *The moon was a cold eye in the sky's sullen face, and branches, bare as winter, made black lines on its brightness.*

◁ 1B Story openings ▣

Answers for the types of opening may vary. Examples:
1 Question   2 Dramatic   3 and 4 Introducing character and intriguing reader   5 Question

Sentence 1: Underline the words that are necessary to meaning in one colour and those that can be taken out in another colour.

Sentences 2–4: Change the order of the words in these sentences, thinking about the different effect you have created.

Sentences 5–9: Categorize and imitate these sentences in the same way as you did for the OHT sentences.

1 THE MOON was a cold eye in the sky's sullen face, and branches, bare as winter, made black lines on its brightness.

The Shaman's Stone by Hugh Scott, Andersen Press 1988

2 *When Granny Diamond took Joe into the small back-bedroom his heart sank.*

The Owl Tree by Jenny Nimmo, Walker Books 1997

3 The sheep had been brought down from the mountains, because the year was dwindling; winter would soon be here.

Go saddle the sea by Joan Aiken, Jonathan Cape 1978

4 Frank and Jess thought OWN BACK LTD was an excellent idea when they first invented it.

Wilkins' Tooth by Diana Wynne Jones, Macmillan 1973

5 It was the day for choosing a hero.

Krindlekrax by Philip Ridley, Jonathan Cape 1991

6 **They call me Ninny.**

Ninny's Boat by Clive King, Kestrel 1980

7 'Mum! Look! That one!'

Who says animals don't have rights? by Jean Ure, Puffin 1994

8 It was horrible.

The Creeper by Pete Johnson, Corgi Yearling 2000

9 'Snubby!' called a cross voice. 'Snubby! Didn't I tell you to tie Loony up?'

The Rubadub Mystery by Enid Blyton, Collins 1951

Story openings

Read these story openings carefully. Categorize each one and imitate it by writing a similar opening in the space underneath.

1 *How does one describe Artemis Fowl?*

Artemis Fowl by Eoin Colfer, Viking 2001

Type of opening: _____

My version: _____

2 THE TIGER padded through the night.

Secret Heart by David Almond, Hodder Children's Books 2001

Type of opening: _____

My version: _____

3 Nathan Wheatear hated his uncle Jago and could not remember a time he didn't.

The tower at Moonville by Stephen Elboz, Oxford 1999

Type of opening: _____

My version: _____

4 **OK, I admit it – I worry.**

I'm telling you, they're aliens by Jeremy Strong, Puffin 2000

Type of opening: _____

My version: _____

5 'What's wrong?' asked the woodcutter.

Short by Kevin Crossley-Holland, Oxford 1998

Type of opening: _____

My version: _____

Choose interesting words to add colour

When you are writing, choose your adjectives and adverbs carefully.

Do not use too many and avoid repetition – *I saw a <u>large, marmalade, soft, fluffy, weary, silent, sleepy</u> cat.*

Do not use ones that are not needed – *I saw the <u>red</u> letterbox.*

Use them when they add in new information – *I stared at the <u>broken</u> letterbox.*

Try unusual or surprising adjectives or adverbs – *She spoke <u>sarcastically</u>.*

Sometimes you can use a phrase – *the <u>tall and handsome</u> warrior…*

Experiment with sentence order for effect

Sometimes there are different ways to order the words in a sentence. Think about the effect this may have on the reader.

For instance, you can move adverbs:
   She walked slowly.
   Slowly, she walked.

You can move prepositional phrases:
   She walked to the end of the road.
   To the end of the road, she walked.

Remember – if you start a sentence with an adverb or a prepositional phrase, use a comma after it.

Write effective openings for your stories

The opening is possibly the most important moment in the story – because if it does not interest your reader, and make them want to read on, your story may never be read!

So, make your openings interesting!

These are different sorts of opening that you can use:

- dramatic statement: *The bomb exploded without warning at half past two.*
- exclamation: *'Come back!' yelled Mr Potter.*
- looking back to a key event: *It had been only a week ago that Sim had discovered the cave.*
- straight into the action: *The two girls screamed.*
- main character makes an error: *Without thinking, I stretched out and stole the orange.*
- dialogue – question opening: *'Where are you going to?' asked Mrs Savage.*
- atmospheric scene setting: *The wind whipped round the crumbling tower.*

When you are reading and like an opening, notice how it is written. Imitate it by writing one that is similar. Add this to your collection of possible openings for your own writing.

UNIT 2

Using standard English

The purpose of this unit is for pupils to think about the basic conventions of standard English, and when it should be used. The children have to consider any local variations, and distinguish between what we may say and what we write when using standard English. This topic should be revisited in terms 2 and 3.

NLS coverage

Key objective

SL 2 To understand the basic conventions of standard English and to consider when and why standard English is used: agreement between nouns and verbs; consistency of tense and subject; avoidance of double negatives; avoidance of non-standard dialect words

Learned through:

TL Reading comprehension
3 To investigate how characters are presented through dialogue, action and description

Assessment criteria

SL By the end of this unit, pupils should be able to identify when standard English is not used in writing; understand the most common variations between local dialect and standard English.

TL Writing composition
Children should be able to write dialogue that reflects local dialect or standard English to aid characterization.

Session 1

You will need OHT 2 and PCM 2A.

Shared reading

1 Read through the top half of the OHT. What do the children notice about the writing? How does it make the writing sound? Who are the main characters – what might be going on? How do you know something about the characters? – through what they say, what they do or how they look.

2 Read through the bottom half. What does the class think the first sentence means? Let them tease this out from the context.

3 How should the speech be spoken? Let several children try saying the dialogue – practise in pairs.

4 What does 'gurt' mean? What sort of word is this? Are there any local words that are similar?

5 What does the class notice about the difference between the narrative and the dialogue?

Sentence level work

1 Cover the bottom half of the OHT. Explain that each sentence is something that someone might say rather than write. Play a game of 'grammar detectives': read the sentences through – who can spot where it 'doesn't sound right', who can explain why the sentence is not in standard English?

2 Ask children, in pairs, to alter each sentence into standard English.

3 Start off the following list on the board. As a class, add examples of common alternatives.

Some people say in local speech:	In standard English we say or write:
real quick	*quickly*

In particular, watch out for the following:
- adjectives used as adverbs, e.g. *he ran real quick*
- subject-verb agreement with *was/were*, e.g. *he were, they was*
- *them* used as a determiner, e.g. *them cows*
- double negatives, e.g. *we didn't say nothing to no-one*
- use of *what/as* as relative pronouns, e.g. *the car what/as I bought*
- incorrect past tense, e.g. *we buyed it.*

4 Add to this list any examples from local dialect.

5 Now uncover the bottom half of the OHT. Read through the extract from *Cider With Rosie*. Distinguish between the accent and the grammatical structures. (You can talk in any accent but still speak standard English.) In pairs, let the children convert what is said into standard English. How does this alter the flavour of the passage?

Independent activities

Direct pupils to PCM 2A. Read through the text together. The children have to underline the places where non-standard English has been used and alter the sentences so that they are in standard English.

Plenary

Read through the original extract and then listen to suggestions. Focus on ensuring that the children have identified the places where a non-standard form is used and can change it to standard. Discuss how different it makes the passage – and the characters – sound.

Session 2

You will need pupils' book 3, Unit 2, pages 10–11, and PCM 2B.

Shared reading

Read the passage through. This may need several readings and can be fun if a number of pupils take different parts with the teacher as narrator. Discuss the following points:

- What do we know about the Snargets?
- How does the author develop their characters? Find words or phrases that help to build up the picture through
  – what they say
  – how they say it
  – what they do
  – description
  – Barney's response.
- Make a class list of the clues that the author uses to build up the characterization.
- Point out that there is very little description – in the main, characterization is accomplished through what characters say, how they say it, and what they do.

Sentence level work

Discuss places in the Snargets' speech where the spelling suggests accent, e.g. *yer* instead of *your*. Find places where the spelling or sentence construction reflect non-standard English, e.g. *ain't*; *What was you*

doin' in our shack? Look at the sentence *I'm the Lone Ranger, and 'e's Robin Hood and 'e's William Tell.* This sentence is grammatically in standard English, though the spelling suggests a different accent. Draw children's attention to the idea that, when developing characters, in can be useful to use a local dialect as this may make them sound real.

Independent activities

Children complete questions A and B in the pupils' book. For those pupils who may find the Snargets' use of dialect demanding, begin by using PCM 2B: in this there is a series of sentences. Children complete the chart to show the non-standard and standard (posh) forms. Once they have done this, they should work in pairs on the tasks in the pupils' book.

Plenary

Use the plenary to tease out where non-standard forms have been used. Reread the whole piece, with no alteration because of accent or non-standard forms, and listen to the way in which it makes the passage very different. Discuss how it seems to alter the Snargets' characters.

Session 3

You will need pupils' book 3, Unit 2, pages 10–11, and the Reminder Sheet.

Shared writing

Revisit basic ideas about characterization and standard English from the Reminder Sheet. For example:

- find a good name
- think about how the character feels or what sort of person they are
- when you are writing, balance action and dialogue with limited description
- use dialect to help build realistic characterization for at least one character
- collect and use stock phrases and local expressions
- draw the children's attention back to any particular non-standard forms that they often use inappropriately in their writing.

Write together

1 Explain that you are going to continue the conversation between Barney and the chief Snarget, aiming to contrast the two by using different dialects. First, make a short list of possible local expressions or non-standard forms that the chief Snarget might use.

2 Ask the children, in pairs, to spend several minutes rehearsing the possible discussion, following on from the end of the passage. Children take it in turns to be Barney.

3 Use one – or several – examples as a basis for the shared writing. Demonstrate several lines yourself, e.g.
'Well, I am going to get Stig,' declared Barney, staring at the oldest Snarget. There was a pause.
'Oh no you ain't,' replied the smallest Snarget. Barney gulped as the Snargets laughed.

Independent writing activity

The class work in pairs on developing the text further. It may be useful to give them several prompts to guide their composition, e.g.

■ Barney and the chief Snarget argue for a little longer
■ Barney says that Stig knows how to fight
■ the chief mocks this
■ Barney gives them one last chance to leave
■ the Snargets poke fun at him
■ Barney tries to leave to find Stig
■ the chief blocks his way
■ Stig appears
■ the Snargets flee.

Plenary

Give a little time for the children to work in pairs preparing a reading of their dialogue. When listening, draw attention to any places where local dialect has been successfully used to reflect character or lend an air of reality to the dialogue. Look for contrasts between the use of standard and non-standard English between Barney and the chief Snarget.

Session 4

You will need a section of work you have written, and/or a selection written by pupils, on OHT, and the Reminder Sheet.

Shared writing

You may find that some pupils have produced a string of dialogue that sounds like a TV script. Show an example of this. Begin by highlighting any successful places where a contrast between Barney and the chief Snarget has been achieved by using different dialects. Then identify where the dialogue has just become a stream of what is said.

Write together

1 Demonstrate how this can be improved by adding between what is said:
■ what the speaker does as he is speaking
■ how the listener reacts.
    For instance, the following exchange could be improved as a model.
    'Wot's this 'ere Stig got that's so speshul, then?' said the chief.
    'He is stronger than you are,' replied Barney.

2 Demonstrate how to 'infill' between what is said. For instance,
'Wot's this 'ere Stig got that's so speshul, then?' said the chief, turning to grin at his brothers. He winked at the youngest and turned back to Barney, flexing his arm muscles. Barney swallowed.
'He is stronger than you are,' replied Barney.

Independent writing activity

Ask the children to take several places in their writing and 'infill' in the same way, thinking about how the different characters might respond. Remind them to focus on adding in:
■ what the speaker does
■ how the listener responds.
More able writers can add in other descriptive detail, for example:
The two boys glared at each other. Bees droned in the hollyhocks and the sun blazed. Nobody spoke for a while.

Plenary

Take several examples – especially where work has been written straight onto OHT. Listen to the original and then the final draft, where the dialogue has been embellished with some 'infilling'. End the session by discussing the use of non-standard forms to help dialogue sound realistic. Make a quick list of types of writing where standard English is vital, e.g. formal letters, reports, essays; and another list where it might be inappropriate, e.g. chatting to friends.

Assessment

Pupils should be able to:
• compose some dialogue using local dialect and non-standard forms in order to build up characterization
• identify common non-standard forms and turn them into standard English
• build character through action, dialogue and limited description.

Model answers

Pupils' book 3 ☐ **A**

1 They have been playing a game using these names. They don't want Barney to know who they are.
2 He pretends not to mind; tells them that they wouldn't dare; says he will tell a policeman, his Granny or Stig.
3 He's putting a brave face on events.
4 They think that a Granny wouldn't be much of a threat to them.

Pupils' book 3 ☐ **B**

5 *yer, 'e's, doin', watcher, chickin', wiv, 'im.*
6 e.g.
'Yes, and what are you doing in our dump anyway?' piped the youngest fiercely.
'Can if I want to,' replied Barney, pretending not to mind. But he was not really feeling very comfortable. He was not sure just how rough these Snargets could get.

' *"Can if he wants to!", he says!' exclaimed the Lone Ranger as if he couldn't believe his ears. 'What shall we do with him, fellows?'*
'Tie him to a tree and shoot him full of arrows,' suggested Robin Hood.
'Put him in a dungeon and leave him to rot,' said William Tell.
'No, I reckon we ought to lynch him on the spot. String him up!' said the Lone Ranger masterfully.
'We have not got any rope,' said Robin Hood.
7 *We ain't got no rope. What was you doin' in our shack?*

☐ **2A   Using standard English** ⌶

Check that children can identify non standard usage, e.g. *I go round to <u>me</u> Nan's = I go round to my Nan's.*

☐ **2B   Dialogue in local dialect** ⌶

we seen/saw; *I never took nothing* / I didn't take anything; *you was*/were; *really likes*/like; *them watches*/those.

Put it right!

Read these sentences through and underline the places where non-standard English has been used. Alter the sentences so that they are in standard English.

I never do nothing when I go round to me Nan's.

She ate her veggie burger dead fast.

They was running down the snicket like a herd of wildebeest.

The car what I was driving was green as the grass in our back yard!

When we got up close, we realized that the dinosaur was big like.

We really likes it when we go down to the town and go to the cinema.

'Listen Terry, I seen her running down past the supermarket on Kyton's Way.'

The card player was dead quick with his hands, faster than a rattle-snake.

'Put them bags down Mister!' snarled Jake O'Leary.

Making dialogue interesting

Read these sentences. Complete the chart to show the non-standard and standard forms.

> 'Jo, we seen you making faces at Mrs Smithers,' snapped Sim. He stared at his sister. Her face tightened as she glared back.
>
> 'I never took nothing from her,' snarled Jo. She whirled round and made for the door. But Sim was quicker and blocked the way.
>
> 'You was seen!' came back the reply, like machine-gun fire.
>
> Jo smiled. She moved slowly towards the door, like a snake trying to hypnotise its prey.
>
> 'I really likes it when you sound cross, Sim,' she giggled. But Sim was not going to be fooled.
>
> 'You put them watches down here,' he said calmly, pointing to the table. Jo looked down at the stolen watches. They would fetch a good price, she knew.

Non-standard English	Standard English
We seen	*We saw*

2 — *Using standard English*

Standard English

Standard English is the appropriate way to speak and write in most formal situations. Wherever you live, there will be some local ways of saying things that are different from standard English. You need to be aware of these so that you can make the right choices for the right occasions.

Some of the most common non-standard forms to look out for are:

- changes in verbs, e.g. *I seen her.*
- using adjectives as adverbs, e.g. *he ran dead fast.*
- muddling agreement, e.g. *we was, they was.*
- using 'them' inappropriately, e.g. *them books over there.*
- muddling negatives, e.g. *I didn't do nothing.*
- using 'what' inappropriately, e.g. *the pencil what is mine.*

Add any other local forms:

Characterization

Non-standard forms can be useful when writing plays and dialogue. It can help your characters to sound realistic. Collect local expressions and ways of saying things. When watching TV, take notes of expressions from around the country that might be useful. Listen to how people speak and use this when writing.

When building your characters think about the following:

- Name: choose a good name, e.g. Lanky O'Legs.
- Description: limit this to one or two things that suggest something about the character, e.g. he has a glass eye.
- Type: decide how the character is feeling or what 'type' of person they are, e.g. a bully.
- When writing, use what the character *says* and *does* to help build character.
- Balance action, dialogue and a limited amount of description. Try to 'infill' between dialogue to avoid a stream of speech. Write what the speaker does and how the listener responds, for example:

'Clear off,' screeched Mrs Savage, pointing at the doorway. The boys slouched across the room.
'We're dead sorry,' muttered Tom.

Improving your writing

The purpose of this unit is to develop pupils' ability to check and improve their own writing. It acts as a useful introduction to revision and establishes a routine that should be followed throughout the year. It links to previous work on proof-reading.

NLS coverage

Key objective

SL 3 To discuss, proof-read and edit their own writing for clarity and correctness, e.g. by creating more complex sentences, using a range of connectives, simplifying clumsy constructions

Learned through:

TL Writing composition
15 To write new scenes or characters into a story, in the manner of the writer, maintaining consistency of character and style, using paragraphs to organize and develop detail

WL 1 To identify mis-spelt words in own writing

Assessment criteria

SL By the end of this unit, pupils should be able to improve their own writing by editing and check for accuracy.

TL Writing composition
Children should be able to develop character through action, dialogue, description and the reactions of other characters.

Session 1

You will need OHT 3, different coloured OHT pens, PCM 3A, and the Reminder Sheet.

Shared reading

Display OHT 3 but mask it so that only the top sentence shows. Read it through. What does this sentence tell us about the man? What does it tell us about the character 'I'? Briefly make the point that some description can help the reader build up a picture of a character. Who can remember other ways of building character? Quickly recap 'action', 'dialogue', 'description', and add on to the list 'other characters' reactions'.

Sentence level work

1 In pairs, ask the children to quickly discuss and, on their whiteboard, to trim the first sentence right back to its bare bones. On the OHT:

2 Use one colour to underline the descriptive lists: *big, curly, white / small, round, gold.*

3 Underline where the clause *a bit startled* has been dropped into *I turned to see.* Discuss other ideas for what might have been 'dropped in', e.g. *I turned, grinning crazily, to see…*

4 Use the second sentence to discuss possible ways to improve – children might write different versions on whiteboards or in notebooks. They could try:
- extending the sentence
- using extra description
- dropping in a phrase or clause.

5 Now read through from *Sian went through…* down to *… scattering down the road.* As a class, work on the first sentence to improve it. You could:
- extend the sentence (at the beginning or end)
- add in description
- drop in a clause or phrase
- use a powerful verb.

6 Discuss and share ideas. Now work on each sentence in turn. Reveal the bottom section of the OHT, drawing attention to the alterations. Notice, for instance, where extra pieces of information have been dropped into the sentences.

Independent activities

Direct pupils to PCM 3A. Read the sentences through. Use the checklist of things that might be done to a sentence on the Reminder Sheet. Try to make the characters and their actions more vivid:

- drop in words, a clause or a phrase, to enrich the description
- extend the sentences
- change words for effect
- rewrite or trim sentences, or parts of sentences.

Before the children begin, work on the first sentence together. Try to use the revision to bring the character alive.

Plenary

Listen to different options. Ask the children which sentences are most effective in bringing the character alive. Then ask them to identify how this has been done.

Session 2

You will need pupils' book 3, Unit 3, pages 12–13, a photocopy for each pupil of the extract from *Crummy Mummy and Me*, PCM 3B, and the Reminder Sheet.

Shared reading

1 Read through the passage on page 12 of the pupils' book. How does the author fool the reader?

2 Discuss what we know about Mina's character – where are the clues? What do we know about Crummy Mummy, and where are the clues? How is the author building up their characters?

Sentence level work

1 Using the photocopy, read through the passage again and underline effective use of words, phrases and clauses that add extra detail, powerful words, interesting expressions.

2 Look at the sentence *She'll sail down in midwinter, when it's snowing, in a thin cotton frock with short puffy sleeves, and no woolly.* Underline the main clause in one colour and pick out the subordinate clause that has been 'dropped in'. Quickly brainstorm together other possible clauses that might have been dropped in.

3 Look at the balance of longer, elaborate sentences mingled with shorter, punchy sentences for effect and clarity.

Independent activities

1 Children complete questions A and B in the pupils' book.

2 Introduce PCM 3B – pretend that this is the first draft of a scene in a story. The task is to discover different ways in which it might be improved. To build up stronger characterization the children could:

- drop in some extra description
- extend sentences to add in more detail
- change weak words for more powerful vocabulary
- rewrite or trim sentences, or parts of sentences that are weak.

Before the children begin, read the text through and work on the opening sentence. The Reminder Sheet has some useful prompts.

Plenary

Use the plenary to listen to several examples. Take each sentence at a time and revise as a class. Remember to focus on improvements that really help build up the character.

Session 3

You will need pupils' book 3, Unit 3, pages 12–13, and the Reminder Sheet.

Shared writing

Explain that the task is to rewrite the first paragraph of 'Crummy Mummy and Me' to alter the impact of the writing, thinking about characterization. Revisit the checklist of possible ways of varying sentences:

- drop in some extra description
- extend sentences to add in more detail
- change weak words for more powerful vocabulary
- rewrite or trim sentences, or parts of sentences that are weak.

Write together

You might wish to demonstrate the first few sentences and then involve the children. For example:

At long last, she trails downstairs. Even then she is never dressed properly. Honestly, you'd think that we didn't have any windows upstairs. Well, look at what she chooses to wear. She certainly can't bother to look through them at the weather. I mean, she sails down in midwinter, with the snow thick as a duvet, dressed in the thinnest cotton frock with short puffy sleeves. Not a woolly in sight!

As you write you could make the following points:

- the style is kept chatty
- the weak verb *comes* is strengthened to *trails*

- the third sentence is reordered to emphasize the word *honestly*
- the third sentence is changed into two shorter ones, for greater emphasis
- *I mean* is used to enliven the chatty style
- a simile (*thick as a duvet*) is used to enrich the description
- the end of the last sentence is turned into a sentence fragment, and made into an exclamation, for impact.

Independent writing activity

The task for the children is to write another incident with the roles reversed – only several paragraphs. In the pupils' book, several suggestions are made. Brainstorm ideas with the class, e.g. Crummy Mummy wants to ride her new scooter on the road and Mina will not let her as it is dangerous. Emphasize the need for the children to keep rehearsing sentences, trying them in different ways and rereading to see if they could be improved. It helps to reread the original model as this sets the style that has to be imitated.

Plenary

Listen to a few examples – does the writer manage the role reversal? Identify effective sentences that bring characters or their actions alive.

Session 4

Use the section of work below plus the Reminder Sheet.

Shared writing

Demonstrate how this first draft might be improved, using the Reminder Sheet to prompt possible developments.

First draft

Well, she's sitting there with her feet up on the table, with her shoes on, watching the TV. I give her one of my looks. But it's no good. She's chewing gum as well. Now, I can't stand gum chewing. But it's even worse than that. She takes the gum out and sticks it to the bottom of the table. I bend down and there's a whole row of chewing gum stuck there. If that isn't bad enough, she turns the volume up so loud that I cannot hear myself think.

Possible improvements

*Well, she's sitting there with her **clumpy** feet **plonked** on the **kitchen** table, with her **muddy Nike trainers** on, watching **'Neighbours'**. So I give her one of my **fiercest glares**. But it's no good. She's chewing gum, **with her mouth wide open.** Now, I can't stand gum chewing. But it's even worse than that. She **spits** a **lump** of **grey gum** out and sticks it under the table. I bend down and there's a whole row of **grey chewing gum stuck** there. **You can see the old tooth prints.** And, if that isn't bad enough, she turns the volume up so loud that I cannot hear myself think.*

Write together

Take sentences from a few pupils and, as a class, improve them. Select pieces that hold common weaknesses, e.g. weak verbs, clumsy or lengthy sentences, too many words used, where reordering would help, a place where a clause might be dropped in.

Independent writing activity

Ask pupils to work in pairs, taking it in turns to improve each other's work. Once improvements have been made, they should check for punctuation and spelling errors, using a dictionary or spellcheck to ensure accuracy.

Plenary

Listen to improved versions. End by summarizing what has been learned.

Assessment

Pupils should be able to:
- discuss, proof-read and improve their own writing, making sensible alterations
- write a new scene in a story, imitating the writer, maintaining consistency of character and style.

Model answers

Pupils' book 3 ☐ **A**

1 Her clothes are impractical for the weather; she'll get cold; she might wear the wrong item for an occasion; she doesn't look the part.

2 Various possible ideas, e.g. she might make her mum feel bad about herself.

3 It's a comical way of suggesting that she is not very good at being a mother.

Pupils' book 3 ☐ **B**

4a *I just stare at her.*

4b *She'd rather wear those baggy flowery shorts than anything sensible.*

Sentence (b) can be rewritten in various ways, e.g.
'She'd rather wear those baggy flowery shorts than anything sensible, if she were called in to see the headmaster.'
or
'Rather than anything sensible, if she were called in to see the headmaster, she'd wear those baggy flowery shorts.'

☐ **3A** and **3B** Improving your writing ▯

Various possible responses – check they are improvements!

Rewrite these sentences to make the characters, or their actions, more interesting.

Work on the first sentence as a class. Then try sentences 2–5.

Sentence 1 – improve by dropping in words and a clause.

Sentence 2 – extend the sentence at the beginning and end.

Sentence 3 – change weak words.

Sentence 4 – reorder the sentence.

Sentence 5 – trim this clumsy sentence.

1 The man went to the shop.

_____

_____

2 The girl laughed.

_____

_____

3 The woman ate some food and looked at the car.

_____

_____

4 The marathon runner skidded crazily across the road without warning.

_____

_____

5 The mad dog grabbed the alien by the leg and, although the alien tried its best, the dog got the alien and gave the alien's leg a bite that made the alien scream in pain.

_____

_____

Read this first draft of a paragraph – it is rather dull! Can you improve it?
Look at the Reminder Sheet for ideas.

Sandy went downstairs. She waited for her Dad. There was a silence. She could just hear him moving about in his bedroom. What on earth was he doing? At that moment the door burst open. He came out. He was dressed in jeans and a tee shirt. His hair was not tidy. He had on his shoes. He looked at Sandy. He came downstairs. They went outside.

3 Improving your writing

When you start writing there are two important things to think about:

1 What sort of writing is this?
2 Who am I writing for?

The answers to these two questions will help you choose the right style.

As you are writing, keep choosing words carefully and think about how the sentences sound. It helps to make the sentence up and listen to it in your own head. This means that you can alter it before you write it down.

Once you have finished writing, check it over. You are looking for three things:

1 Can the writing be improved?
2 Is the punctuation accurate?
3 Is the spelling correct?

Improving your sentences

Take the sentence *The robber ran quickly*. You could work on this as follows:

1 Drop in well chosen words, e.g.
   The cheerful robber ran crazily.

2 Drop in a clause, e.g.
   The robber, who was laughing like a madman, ran quickly.
   The robber, startled by the police, ran.

3 Extend the sentence at the beginning, e.g.
   Although he was not being chased, the robber ran quickly.

4 Extend the sentence at the end, e.g.
   The robber ran quickly because the crocodile was chasing him.

5 Change weak words, e.g.
   The robber rushed.

6 Reorder the sentence, e.g.
   Quickly, the robber ran.

7 Finally, trim long and clumsy sentences to make your writing punchy, e.g.
   The robber, who was laughing like a madman, ran quickly because the crocodile was chasing him.
   becomes:
   The robber ran!

Characterization

Remember – you can build up a character by showing what another person thinks of them.

UNIT 4

Adapting a playscript

The purpose of this unit is to help pupils think about how they might adapt different types of writing, adjusting their style and taking account of the audience and purpose.

NLS coverage

Key objective

SL 4 To adapt writing for different readers and purposes by changing vocabulary, tone and sentence structures to suit, e.g. simplifying for younger readers

Learned through

TL Reading comprehension
5 To understand the conventions of scripting a play

Assessment criteria

SL By the end of this unit, pupils should be able to think about how writing needs to be adapted according to audience and purpose.

TL Children should understand the basic conventions for writing a scene from a play.

Session 1

You will need OHT 4 and PCM 4A.

Shared reading

1 Display OHT 4, covering the bottom half so that only the play extract can be seen. Read it through – what sort of writing is this? List the conventions. How does the audience know what is happening? Make the point that much of the description does not have to be written down as the audience will be able to see the characters and set on stage.

2 Make a list of what we know about the teacher and the girls.

3 Reveal the bottom section of the OHT, where the play is translated into narrative. Underline the parts that are from the play (the speech and the stage directions).

4 Discuss how much more the story has added. Find instances where our understanding is deepened in the story. Add to the list anything extra that we now know.

Sentence level work

Working as a class, take the opening to the play. Rewrite it in a different manner, making the teacher

sound curious, as if the girls are doing something interesting. For example:

Mr Fountain bounced into the classroom. He had only two lessons to go before the end of the day and then he would be leaving Grange Primary School. He noticed Tracy and Joanne, two of his favourite pupils, working hard at building a magnificent sculpture.

'What on earth are you up to?' he asked, staring in amazement at the papier mâché palace. The girls stared at him.

'Nothing,' gasped Tracy. They were building a present for Mr Fountain and it was vital that he should not guess the surprise.

Independent activities

Direct pupils to PCM 4A. The task is to read the few lines from the play and then turn them into a story. The opening sentences are done. Those who finish early could try adapting the writing in different ways, e.g. rewriting it as if it was a diary entry or a letter to a friend about the incident.

Plenary

Listen to various examples. Draw children's attention to the way in which the text sounds different, especially to the amount of extra description that is needed.

Session 2

You will need pupils' book 3, Unit 4, pages 14–15, and PCM 4B.

Shared reading

1 Read through the extract 'A cut too far!'

2 Discuss what has happened – How do the different characters feel? How do you know? Who do you think did it, and why?

Sentence level work

Look carefully at the basic conventions of writing a playscript – ask the children to work these out and make a list.

- Character's name in bold
- Space between name and what is said
- No use of speech marks
- Occasional directions in italics and brackets
- Everything has to be understood through the speech.
- A play is like a story with only the dialogue.

Independent activities

Children complete questions A and B in the pupils' book. Provide sufficient time for them to practise a decent performance. You may need to help some children adapt the play into another form of writing – just give brief starters on a board to help them use the right style. Use PCM 4B for early finishers. In this, sentences have to be altered to fit a different sort of text type.

Plenary

Use the plenary to hear some of the prepared readings. Discuss as a class the key factors in performing from a script. For example:

- make sure everyone can hear the words
- do not read too quickly
- use expression
- think about the audience!

Session 3

You will need pupils' book 3, Unit 4, pages 14–15, and the Reminder Sheet.

Shared writing

Reread the playscript and introduce the task – to rewrite the play as a story. To help, begin by demonstrating how the opening might be rewritten. For example:

Daisy raced out of her bedroom onto the landing, her face flushed with anger. In her hand she clutched Fiona, her favourite Barbie doll.
'Right, which of you is responsible?' she barked. Poppy stared at Tony and Tony stared at the doll. The doll was bald, quite bald. Someone had shaved it and they were about to get the blame.
Poppy swallowed. 'Not me,' she stammered.

Write together

Move on to adapting the next few lines from the play. Add in extra detail and description. If it helps, ask some children to act out the lines and use this as a basis, asking the children to think about what the characters do as they speak or listen – and what they are feeling.

Independent writing activity

Set the task given in the pupils' book. Just before the children write, ask a group to perform the scene once more to help the class visualize what they are going to write.

Plenary

Listen to several examples. Ask the children to check that the lines from the play are included. Identify extra pieces of description that help the reader to visualize the characters and what they are doing, and to know what they are feeling.

Session 4

You will need a section of work you have written, or one written by a pupil, on OHT, and the Reminder Sheet.

Shared writing

Remind pupils of the focus – adapting playwriting to narrative, and thinking about how this affects what to include.

Write together

Use the following weak version. Work as a class to improve it by adding in more description that shows what is happening and what the characters feel.

'OK. I'll go and find Mum. Mum, Mum!' said Daisy. Mum came in.
'What is that dreadful shouting for?' she said.
'Somebody's ruined my Barbie,' said Daisy, feeling sad.
Mum looked at Daisy's brother and sister. Mum said, 'Right you two. Who did this?' The children did not answer.

Independent writing activity

Ask the children to work in threes and take it in turns to read aloud their stories. After each reading, the others should comment on:

- what they liked
- one place that might be improved.

Provide time for improvements to be made in the light of comments. Anyone who completed the task very successfully first time round could be asked to rewrite the scene as if it were in diary form, taking the role of one of the children or the mother.

Plenary

Listen to improved versions. Note different ways of showing how the characters think and feel through their reactions, for instance, or reveal what is going on in their heads.

Assessment

Pupils should be able to:

- think about how writing can be adapted for a different purpose or audience by altering the style
- understand the basic conventions of a play.

Model answers

Pupils' book 3 ◻ A

1 Someone has shaved the hair off Daisy's doll.
2 The opening stage direction provides the clue.
3 Poppy.
4 She offers Daisy one of her dolls.

Pupils' book 3 ◻ B

6 e.g. *I stormed into the room, holding up a Barbie doll and asked them who had done it. Of course, they both denied it.*
7 e.g. *So, I turned to Daisy and suggested that her friend Hayley might have done it. I mean, Hayley's always been jealous of Daisy and isn't really a good friend – though Daisy thinks she is. I know they had an argument earlier and Daisy had left her alone in her room so she could have done it.*
8 e.g. *Bald Doll Mystery* or *Barbie Shocker*
9 Remember to check that the presentational features are accurate – and that the characters are well delineated.

◻ 4A Adapting a playscript ▯

Ensure that children's writing sounds like narrative. They need to add in background – what characters do as they speak plus other aspects from the setting.

◻ 4B Adapting writing ▯

The key is for each sentence to 'sound' as if it came from the type of writing suggested.

Turn this scene from a play into a story. The opening sentence is done for you.

Scene 3

Sandy	Let's go down to the canal.
Simmy	You know I can't. My Mum would kill me!
Sandy	You're such a baby, Simmy. Do you have to do what Mummy says?
Simmy	No, it's just that…
Sandy	Just what?
Simmy	Well, since my Dad left home I don't like to cross my Mum.
Sandy	Well, if you're not going, I am…

Sandy grabbed Simmy by the arm and tugged at her sleeve. 'Let's go down to the canal,' she said eagerly. There was a new boat at the lock and that might mean that they could sell some of Mrs Marvin's flowers. But Simmy stared back, uncertain.

   'You know I can't…

_____

_____

_____

_____

_____

_____

_____

_____

Change the sentence into different text types. The first is done for you.

The Prime Minister spilled gravy on his new shirt.

1 Traditional tale

Example: ONCE UPON A TIME there
was a Prime Minister who
spilled gravy onto his shirt.

2 Mystery story

_____

_____

3 Play

_____

_____

4 Note to the drycleaners

_____

_____

5 Newspaper report

_____

_____

6 Prime Minister's diary

_____

_____

7 Advert

_____

_____

4 | *Adapting a playscript*

Adapting writing

Always think carefully about who you are writing for (the audience) and what you are trying to achieve (the purpose) as this will influence your writing.

Think about the type of writing that you are doing. It is helpful if you have a good example to look at. This will remind you of the style – the sort of words that are used, how the sentences sound. For instance, instructions sound very different from a newspaper report:

Place the cat firmly on the mat. (instruction)

Last night a cat was seen by Mrs Harrison, aged 48, sitting on a mat. (newspaper report)

If you muddle your style and use the wrong sort of language in the wrong place, it can sound very odd! For example:

The Prime Minister said, 'Your majesty, how about a nice bit of dead good ketchup on your spuds, and then we'll all get set for a bit of break-dancing, eh?'

Writing plays

Plays are like stories – but you only need to write down what is said. You can include a few stage directions, which are written in italics inside brackets. Write the name of the person who is speaking on the left-hand side, preferably in bold. Either leave a space between the name and what is said, or use a colon, e.g.

Bill   Where are you?
Bill: Where are you?

When writing a play, you do not need to describe what a person looks like, what they are doing or where they are, because the acting and scenery will show this.

In a play you have to choose carefully what is said, as this is all the actors have to guide them. You cannot reveal what is inside somebody's mind unless you:

- have them thinking aloud
- have other characters discussing what they feel
- show by reactions what people think or feel.

When you write a playscript, it is helpful to get some feedback by acting it out in front of an audience. Putting a scene onto tape and then listening to it is another useful way of judging how well it works.

Direct & reported speech

The purpose of this unit is for pupils to understand the difference between direct and reported speech and to begin using this in writing a recount.

NLS coverage

Key objective

SL 5 To understand the difference between direct and reported speech (e.g. 'she said, "I am going"', 'she said she was going'), through:

- finding and comparing examples from reading
- discussing contexts and reasons for using particular forms and their effects
- transforming direct into reported speech and vice versa, noting changes in punctuation and words that have to be changed or added.

Learned through

TL Writing composition

24 To write recounts based on a subject, topic or personal experiences, e.g. an account of a historical event

Assessment criteria

SL By the end of this unit, pupils should be able to use direct and reported speech effectively.

TL Writing composition

Children should be able to write a recount using reported speech.

Session 1

You will need OHT 5, an OHT pen, and PCM 5A.

Shared reading

1 Display OHT 5, covering the bottom half. Read through the top left-hand column. Which sentences reveal most about the character? How does the author accomplish this?

2 If this was a narrative text, what is missing? It sounds more like a play!

Sentence level work

1 Working in pairs, the children should make two statements about sentences in the left-hand column, e.g. all use speech marks, all have a speech verb.

2 Now look at the right-hand column. What do the children notice?

3 Draw attention to where the word 'that' should be used but is often missed out (shown in brackets).

4 Explain that the left-hand column is called 'direct speech' – this is where whatever the speaker says is shown directly, inside speech marks. The right-hand column is called 'indirect (or 'reported') speech' and this is where the writer 'reports' what was said.

5 Notice how direct speech is converted to reported speech. (Use the same speech verb, start the sentence with, e.g., *he said* – often followed by *that, whether, if, how, to*.)

6 Now reveal the bottom left-hand column. Work as a class to change each sentence into reported speech. Think about the various changes that need making.

Independent activities

Direct pupils to PCM 5A. It contains the same sort of activity as OHT 5 and the children are asked to convert direct speech into indirect speech.

Plenary

Listen to answers and discuss changes that had to be made to the sentences. Discuss when indirect speech might be useful – e.g. in a recount when writing about what has happened.

Session 2

You will need pupils' book 3, Unit 5, pages 16–17, and PCM 5B.

Shared reading

1 Read 'Another Food Upset'. Take initial observations and explain that this text is an extract from a newspaper written in 1837. What clues suggest that the article was written a while ago?
2 Give the children time to discuss the following:
   ■ Who do you think was in the right?
   ■ Was this a fair hearing?
   Ask them to find clues from the text to support their views.

Sentence level work

1 Ask pupils to tell you what sort of text this is. (A newspaper report, or recount of an event.)
2 Ask pupils to look through the text and find examples of direct speech and reported speech.
3 As this is a recount there is bound to be some reported speech. Discuss the sentence construction.

Independent activities

Introduce the pupils' book activities A and B. Changing the text into narrative and using reported speech may need some discussion or a brief example written together. Give PCM 5B to early finishers. On this children have to translate a recount, using reported speech, into a narrative using direct speech.

Plenary

Double-check that children understand the basic difference between direct and reported speech. Reinforce the idea that direct speech makes the drama 'happen'. Reported speech is useful in recounts. Listen to some of the pupils' versions of the first and last paragraphs. Which is most effective, and why?

Session 3

You will need pupils' book 3, Unit 5, pages 16–17, and the Reminder Sheet.

Shared writing

Reread the passage in the pupils' book. Introduce the task – to write Sarah Dunk's defence in the present tense, as if it were actually happening. Before writing, make a list of the points that Sarah might use – refer back to the original to pick up clues, such as the matron having hit her before.

Write together

To tune the children into the use of direct speech, with some reported speech, demonstrate a possible opening of Sarah's defence. For example:

Sarah Dunk stood up and stared at the magistrate. She cleared her throat and spoke. 'Your Honour,' she began, curtseying. 'That morning Matron did not give me any gruel. She told me that I did not deserve it.' There was a pause, and Sarah glared at the Matron. 'She has hit me…'

When writing, put the direct speech in one colour and the reported speech in another to draw attention to the different features.

Independent writing activity

The children continue writing, building on the whole-class beginning. Make sure that there is an adequate list of points that Sarah will make, to support each pupil in writing. Set the challenge that everyone has to use at least one piece of reported speech. They should use the Reminder Sheet as they write.

Plenary

Listen to several examples. Ask the children to identify the places where reported speech is used.

Session 4

You will need the Reminder Sheet.

Shared writing

Remind pupils of the focus – using direct and reported speech. Read aloud or show any effective pieces from the previous day. Build on this by setting the task – to write a brief recount about a time that you were in trouble. Tell pupils to include what happened, what was said – and to use both direct and reported speech.

Write together

Demonstrate a paragraph. You might wish to use the following or invent your own. Make sure that you include both reported and direct speech.

When I was in Year 3 I got into trouble for eating sweets. We had a really strict teacher and she did not allow us to eat in class. One day she saw me chewing.

'What are you eating?' she barked at me. I told her that I was just chewing my tongue.

'In that case you can open your mouth,' she replied. I didn't want to be caught out so I just sat there and pressed my lips together. She told my Mum that I had been eating in class. I got into trouble at home for that.

Independent writing activity

To help the children sort out what they are going to write, ask them to relate a few incidents. They could work in pairs and have a few minutes each to tell their recount. Then listen to a few as a class. Emphasize that you only want a few paragraphs – a brief recount – using some direct and some reported speech.

Plenary

Listen to several examples – ask the class to discuss what they liked and draw attention to the handling of speech.

Model answers

Pupils' book 3 ☐ A

1 The matron gave the most evidence. Various possible reasons, e.g. the poor were not listened to; Sarah was not good at speaking.
2 Various possibilities, e.g. Sarah was starving; they felt sorry for her; she bullied them.
3 She suggests that others urge Sarah to behave in this way.
4 We know that the torn caps were produced as evidence. Maybe others saw the incident though this is not reported. Maybe there was no proper evidence.
5 He sounds tough, as he says that there would be *no dispute about the 'gruel' in his quarters.*

Pupils' book 3 ☐ B

6 *She replied that she would not* = 'I will not give you any of this,' snarled Sarah.
7 e.g. *The matron stood up ready to begin. 'Repeat these words after me,' said the foreman, holding out the Bible. 'I swear to tell the truth so help me God.' Matron muttered the words and from the witness stand eyed the dock. Sarah stood there, defiant to the last.*

   The magistrate cleared his throat, 'Sarah Dunk, you are hereby charged with committing a grievous bodily assault on Saturday morning last upon the personage of the matron of Battle workhouse. How do you answer, guilty or not?'

   There was a silence and then Sarah mumbled, 'Not so, yer worship.' Matron's lips tightened.
8 e.g. *Cook, the keeper, stood up, and stared at the magistrate. He spoke in a loud clear voice, with his hands gripping the edge of the bench, his knuckles whitening. 'There'll be no dispute in my quarters when it comes to "gruel", yer 'onor.' He shifted his gaze to Sarah Dunk and she bowed her head, defeated.*

☐5A   Direct & reported speech ⏸

Check for successful writing of reported speech, e.g. *Sandi shouted to Sal that she should look at the cliffs.*

☐5B   Direct & reported speech ⏸

Discussion should touch on the need for variety plus how direct speech brings narrative alive, as if it is happening (and you can 'do' voices!).

Use the space below each sentence to change the direct speech into reported speech.

'Look at the cliffs,' shouted Sandi to Sal.

_____

'I do not want to look at the budgie,' replied Satish.

_____

'Taking care of budgies,' said Mrs Assam, 'is not a job for careless people.'

_____

_____

'My parrot eats sunflower seeds and bananas,' stammered Siegfried.

_____

_____

'I once kept an eagle in my bedroom,' said Toni.

_____

'Was the eagle a pest?' asked Mr Gruel.

_____

This is a recount about a time that someone got into trouble. Rewrite it in the space below, changing it into a story, using direct speech. The opening is done for you.

Reread both versions. Which sounds more effective, and why?

ONE DAY old Silas grabbed my brother Tom by the hair and told him that he was going to tell our Dad that we had stolen stuff from his place. Tom asked him how he knew and Silas replied that we would soon find out. We stood our ground and shouted at him to let Tom go. He said that he was going to tell our Dad that we had cheeked him. Just then my Dad appeared and he told Silas to leave his kids alone. We scarpered.

Old Silas reached out and grabbed Tom by the hair. 'You've been stealing from my place, and I'm going to tell your Dad,' he snarled. We stopped running and faced him. Tom squirmed, trying to get free.

'How do you know that?' asked Tom, tears starting from his eyes.

_____

_____

_____

_____

_____

_____

_____

_____

Direct speech is when a writer uses the original words that were spoken.
For example:
'Cucumbers are hard to bend double,' said Paulie.

Reported speech is when a writer reports what was said but does not necessarily use the exact words that were spoken. Typically, the writer has to change pronouns and tense, and speech marks are not needed.
For example:
Paulie said that cucumbers were hard to bend.

Direct speech is used in stories. It helps to bring them alive. It is especially powerful if you read the story aloud.

Reported speech can help a writer to avoid using a long stream of direct speech. It can help to move the story along quickly, as you do not have to write down everything that was said. For example:
The Queen said that she agreed and so they left the palace.

Reported speech is useful in recounts to report to the reader what was said. In reported speech you often need to use the word 'that', e.g. *She said <u>that</u> she was hungry.* Sometimes 'that' is missed out, e.g. *She said she was hungry.*

When you change from direct to reported speech, you may need to make a number of changes to the sentences. For instance, in the following sentences a number of changes have been made:
'Are you happy?' asked Sim.
Sim asked if she was happy.

Changes

- The tense has been changed (*are* to *was*)
- A connective has been added (*if*)
- The word order has changed
- The punctuation has been altered.

Using punctuation

The purpose of this unit is for pupils to revisit and consolidate the use of punctuation, especially commas, and to become familiar with use of the semi-colon.

NLS coverage

Key objective

SL 6 To understand the need for punctuation as an aid to the reader, e.g. commas to mark grammatical boundaries; a colon to signal, for example, a list

Learned through

TL **Reading comprehension and writing composition**
1 To analyse the features of a good opening and compare a number of story openings
15 To write new scenes into a story

Assessment criteria

SL By the end of this unit, pupils should be able to use punctuation as a writing tool, e.g. use commas in a list and to build up detail.

TL **Writing composition**
Children should be able to write an atmospheric scene in a story.

Session 1

You will need OHT 6 and PCM 6A.

Shared reading

Display OHT 6 and explain that these are openings to five stories. Read through each passage and discuss.

- Extract 1 – Note the use of an unusual name. How does the author make an impact on the reader? (In the list, the last item is a contrast – to surprise the reader.)
- Extract 2 – How do you think the main character is feeling?
- Extract 3 – How does the author create an impact at the start of this story? (She delays the facts.)
- Extract 4 – What is the author doing in this opening? (Quickly setting the scene)
- Extract 5 – How does the author set the scene for the possibility of an adventure?

Sentence level work

Take each extract in turn and look at the use of punctuation.
- 1 – Note the use of commas in a list. Also, notice how the supporting information, *a preacher*, is added in between commas. Demonstrate how to do this on the board, e.g. *Tom, a butcher, appeared at the window.* Show how this can be extended, e.g. *Tom, a butcher from Glasgow, appeared at the window.* Remind the children that usually you do not use a comma just before the 'and' at the end of a list. Note that the actual list ends with *and two tomatoes.*
- 2 – Notice the use of questions to show what the main character is thinking – this also helps to draw the reader into the character's world.
- 3 & 4 – Look at the use of the semi-colon. Explain that semi-colons can be used in two ways.
  - The more usual use of a semi-colon is to separate two main clauses in a sentence, e.g. *He was only about two inches high; and he had a mouse's sharp nose, …*
  - The other use is to separate items in a list, where the list consists of longer phrases, e.g. *I need a peach; half a pound of herby sausages; and a slice of salami.*
- 5 – Look at the use of brackets.

Independent activities

Direct pupils to PCM 6A on which pupils are asked to practise using commas to add information, to use a semi-colon and brackets. If some children find this difficult, regard this as an opportunity for guided work.

Plenary

Listen to the range of responses, creating ideas as a class.

Session 2

You will need pupils' book 3, Unit 6, pages 18–19, and PCM 6B.

Shared reading

1 Read both passages through. Both use the setting as a main focus. Which creates the stronger picture? What words or phrases help this?

2 Read each passage in turn, commenting on the use of language, especially the way in which both authors pile up the descriptive information.

3 Which is the more effective opening, and why? Ask children, in pairs, to think of several reasons why one is better than the other, justifying their ideas by referring to the text.

Sentence level work

1 Look at the punctuation in the first passage. Notice how the semi-colon is used to introduce extra information. Briefly try imitating the pattern used in the second sentence, e.g.
In sunny weather the streets buzzed with life; the clock tower shimmered in the heat; the park benches sizzled.

2 Look at the punctuation in the second passage. Draw attention to the basic structure of:
■ what I can still hear
■ what I can still see.
Use the same sentence pattern to create a third option:
■ what I can still taste or smell.
For example, *When I close my eyes I can still taste the sharp tang of lemon, the sweetness of strawberries and the bitterness of coffee.*

Independent activities

Children complete questions A and B in the pupils' book. Those who struggle can use PCM 6B which offers more support for writing descriptions using a list.

Plenary

Use the plenary to listen to examples and discuss their impact. Ask children to double-check each other's punctuation before handing work in. Can anyone catch their partner out?

Session 3

You will need pupils' book 3, Unit 6, pages 18–19, and the Reminder Sheet.

Shared writing

Reread the Harper Lee extract. Explain that the task is to write a descriptive passage describing the local area. This could be an opening to a story or chapter, introducing the reader to a new setting. Make three quick lists to help:
■ Things we see in the centre – clock tower, cars, etc.
■ Things we see in summer – heat haze, swallows, etc.
■ Things we see in winter – snow on roof tops, etc.

Write together

Base the shared writing on the Harper Lee text. Refer back to the notes made. On the board, demonstrate the use of the semi-colon. Use verbs powerfully, add in detail and use a simile. For example:
Oakridge is a lively village, but it was a tired place when I knew it. In hot weather the heat shimmered; swallows dived and dipped, past sleeping cats; the children made their way to school, shrieking and yelling. When it snowed the roof tops were covered; everyone struggled up the hill; the roads shone with ice like a skating rink.

Independent writing activity

The children write their own version, based on the extracts in the pupils' book and the model on the board.

Plenary

Listen to a few examples read aloud. Ask the class to identify aspects that are effective – especially where detail has been used.

Session 4

You will need a section of work you have written, or one written by a pupil, on OHT, and the Reminder Sheet.

Shared writing

1 Remind pupils of the focus – writing a setting, using detail that is built up with the help of the semi-colon.

2 Discuss what is effective. Identify where improvements could be made. Check the punctuation.

Write together

Display the following passage (or one written by a pupil) and, as a class, improve it.

Exmouth is a lonely town, but it was a great place when I knew it. When the sun was shining the streets seemed to have loads of life and some cars made a noise and the market stalls had lots of shoppers and dogs slept in corners and children played in the park. When it snowed the snow piled up on street corners; the postman could not get up the hill; cats picked their way with care; cars went on the ice; the wind howled like something and we stayed indoors.

Especially note that the semi-colon makes a more powerful link than 'and'. Also include more effective detail.

Independent writing activity

Working in pairs, the children improve their writing, helping each other.

Plenary

Children report back on aspects that have been improved – reading aloud what their writing originally said, and what it has been changed to.

Assessment

Pupils should be able to:
- use a comma in a list to add in detail
- use a semi-colon to build up a description
- write an effective opening paragraph, building up description of the setting.

Model answers

Pupils' book 3 ▱ **A**

1 The streets became awash with red mud, grass grew on the sidewalks and the court-house seemed to sag.
2 The men's collars drooped by nine o'clock. The women had to take a bath before midday as well in the afternoon, and by night were covered with sweat and talcum powder.
3 The seagulls and the fish.
4 See – the various fish. Hear – the gulls squawking, the slushing of crushed ice, the whirring of the trucks.

Pupils' book 3 ▱ **B**

5 Draw children's attention to the use of the comma in the lists.

▱ **6A** Using punctuation ▯

1 Check for commas, e.g. *Tom, the tallest lad in Year 9, ran over the bridge.*
2 e.g. (a) *It's raining so hard that I could build a boat, put it in the street and sail away.* (b) *My teacher sent me to fetch a French dictionary, some old rulers and two ping pong balls.* (c) *He had a thin, sallow complexion, a bright red nose and beady eyes that glared at me.*
3 e.g. *None of us could think; we had memories of a time long ago, but we are not sure if they really happened and besides we could only think about the birthday.*
4 e.g. *The girls stared. (They were from the school, but we never spoke to them.)*

▱ **6B** Using punctuation ▯

Relate these back to the extract from *The Giant Goldfish Robbery* on page 18 of the pupils' book.

1 Write five new sentences, using commas correctly.

Tom	strode into the classroom	the chef's only helper
Mrs Savage	ran over the bridge	the tallest lad in Year 9
Lanky O'Neil	picked up the slab of stone	a weary soldier from London
Skater	lay in the grass and waited	5a's grim-faced teacher
Anya	began to peel the turnip	the youngest athlete

_____

_____

_____

_____

_____

2 Add some detail to the following openings.

a It's raining so hard that I could _____, put it

_____ and _____

b My teacher sent me to fetch a _____, some

_____ and two _____

c He had a _____, a _____ and

_____

3 Complete this sentence which uses a semi-colon.

None of us could think; we had _____, but

_____ and _____

4 Add some extra information into the brackets.

The girls stared. (They _____, but

_____)

6B Using punctuation

Read the examples. Then finish the sentences below, adding in some ideas of your own.

WHEN I CLOSE MY EYES I can still hear the washing machine grumbling in the corner, the mumbling TV from the downstairs flat and the sharp voice of my father shouting.

When I close my eyes I can still hear the _____,

the _____ and

the _____

I CAN SEE THE TRAFFIC rushing down Smith Lane, the letter box on the corner of the avenue and the crisp packets blowing in the wind like bright leaves.

I can see the _____

the _____

and the _____

like _____

6   *Using punctuation*

Writing story openings that set the scene

The opening of a story must work hard. It has to capture the reader's interest.

In some stories you may want to begin by building up the setting. This helps the reader to picture the scene and creates atmosphere. Here are some techniques that you can use.

1 Drop details about your character into the sentence to give the reader extra information, e.g.

   Bodger Clarke, <u>the lazy milkman from Neeth</u>, made his way up the hill.

2 Use commas in a list and to build up detail, usually in blocks of three, e.g.

   My daddy sent me to the store for a box of macaroni-cheese, some white rice and two tomatoes.

   Across the town I could see the Cliff Hotel with its ancient tower, the seagulls wheeling high above and the sea crashing onto the beach.

   When I close my eyes I can still hear the mad squawking of the seagulls, the slushing noises of the crushed ice and the whirring of the fork-lift trucks.

   It helps to use the senses – listing what you can **see** and **hear** is a useful tactic.

3 Use semi-colons to pile up description.

   When the rain came everyone went indoors; the streets were silent except for the beating rain; the trees moved like strange ghosts; the puddles glistened in the lamplight; the gutters gurgled like an old man gulping medicine.

   It can help to describe the place in different **seasons** or **weather**.

Writing dialogue

The purpose of this unit is to secure children's ability to set out dialogue correctly. It concentrates on the idea that dialogue should reflect character and focuses upon the importance of avoiding an endless stream of dialogue! It links with work carried out in Year 3 term 3.

NLS coverage

Key objective

SL 7 From reading, to understand how dialogue is set out, e.g. on separate lines for alternate speakers in narrative, and the positioning of commas between speech marks

Learned through

TL **Reading comprehension and writing composition**
3 To investigate how characters are presented, referring to the text, through dialogue, action and description
15 To write new scenes or characters into a story

WL 10 To use adverbs to qualify verbs in writing dialogue

Assessment criteria

SL By the end of this unit, pupils should be able to punctuate dialogue correctly; use dialogue to develop characterization; avoid a string of speech by describing what characters do as they speak.

TL **Writing composition**
Children should be able to select powerful speech verbs, use adverbs with speech verbs and balance the use of these features when developing characterization in new scenes.

Session 1

You will need OHT 7 and PCM 7A.

Shared reading

1 Display OHT 7, covering everything up except the top four lines. As you work through the OHT, reveal each section in turn.

2 First block of four lines – Is this good writing? What can you tell me about the characters? Why not?

3 Second block of four lines – What is different? (The speech is more realistic.) But is it good writing? What can you tell me about the characters? What else is needed?

4 Third block of four lines – What can you now tell me about the characters? How did you know?

5 Fourth block of dialogue – Is this better? Make a list of the ways the writer has broken up the dialogue to help the reader build up a picture. For example, he/she has added:

■ description of what the speaker does (*grabbing the dog's collar and…*)
■ a description of the character's feelings (*he bit his bottom lip*)
■ her reactions (*she looked anxiously at her friend*).

Sentence level work

1 Return to the top section. Focus on the punctuation. Ask pupils, in pairs, to draw up a quick list of rules for setting out dialogue.

2 Feedback to the whole class and make a checklist. For example:
■ Start a new line for a new speaker
■ Enclose what is said within the speech marks
■ End with a comma, question mark or exclamation mark – within the speech marks
■ Start 'said' with a small letter.

3 Add other points such as:
■ Use a powerful verb to show how the character feels.

4 Demonstrate how an adverb could be added to 'said' by including adverbs in the first block, e.g. *said Sian quietly.*

5 Make the final point that it sounds odd if you just use 'said'. It sounds odd if you keep using powerful verbs. It also sounds odd if you always use 'said' plus an adverb. The answer is – variation.

Independent activities

Direct pupils to PCM 7A which asks the children to do the following:

- Rewrite the first section, using correct punctuation.
- Rewrite the second section selecting powerful verbs or using adverbs.
- Add some information between what is said, thinking about what each speaker is doing. Draw children's attention to the example given. (This can be prompted by acting out a few actions as you say the dialogue.)

Plenary

1 Begin by checking that everyone has understood and can use the basic punctuation and layout covered in section 1 of PCM 7A.

2 Ask children to read aloud the second section. The acid test is – does it sound effective? Have they overused any one strategy? Agree on what sounds best.

3 Listen to examples of rewritten dialogue for the third section. How successfully have the children managed to describe what the speaker and/or listener are doing?

Session 2

You will need pupils' book 3, Unit 7, pages 20–21, and PCM 7B.

Shared reading

1 Read through and discuss initial reactions to the characters.

2 Make a list of what we know about Joey, Grandma, Mary Alice and Ernie Cowgill – and how we know it.

Sentence level work

Now go back and focus on the use of dialogue. What can be learned from this writer? Read through, discuss and make a checklist. For example:

- Have your characters say interesting things

- Show what the character is feeling, e.g. *The kid's eyes widened.*
- Show what the character does, using a comma and an 'ing' word to start the next part of the sentence (a non-finite verb), e.g. *'Naw,' the kid said, reaching around for the knob on the screen door behind him.*
  On the board, try inventing a few sentences using the same tactic, e.g.
  'Hi,' said Gran, picking up a duster and polishing the spoons.
- Use powerful verbs when they are needed to show how the character feels, e.g. *I croaked.*

Independent activities

Children complete questions A and B in the pupils' book, continuing to build on the idea of showing the speaker's actions or the listener's reactions. Use PCM 7B to further develop the idea of describing what is happening while the characters are talking.

Plenary

Use the plenary to take feedback from the activities. Use PCM 7B to summarize different strategies that can be adopted to avoid writing dialogue as a list.

Session 3

You will need pupils' book 3, Unit 7, pages 20–21, and the Reminder Sheet.

Shared writing

Explain that the task is to write a further episode in which Ernie delivers milk to Grandma. Grandma uses the opportunity to boast about Mary Alice. Pupils should try to keep the characters in role (refer back to the list made about them in Session 2).

Write together

Remind pupils of the strategies that can be used for writing dialogue. You might begin this part of the lesson by giving some time to children working in pairs to develop possible dialogue and action between Ernie and Grandma. As you write bear in mind:

- the punctuation and layout of dialogue
- dialogue reflects character
- dialogue is more readable if the characters say interesting things
- writers should describe what happens in between what is said.

Example: *There was a thud at the door and Ernie appeared. 'Here's the cream,' he muttered, eyeing Grandma cautiously. She glowered back at him. I could see that we were in for another episode of whopping lies.*
'Well it better be ok. The last lot was sour,' she snapped at him. With a shudder, Ernie turned quite white. Mary Alice and I stared at him, waiting to see what would happen.
'Sorry,' he stammered, staring at me.
'Of course, Mary Alice, she's a police trainee,' declared Grandma, pointing at my sister. This was quite obviously untrue but Ernie seemed to believe it. There was a silence while the implications sunk in. A fly buzzed in the kitchen.
'I'd best be off,' mumbled Ernie, edging towards the door.

Independent writing activity

The children write their own versions, possibly drawing on their paired improvisations.

Plenary

Listen to examples. Ask the class to feedback to the writer:
- what worked well
- any point that might be improved.

Session 4

You will need a section of work you have written, or one written by a pupil, on OHT, and the Reminder Sheet.

Shared writing

Remind pupils of the focus – writing a scene that uses dialogue to reflect character, avoiding a string of speech.

Write together
Look at some good examples, analysing why they worked. Demonstrate how to improve common weaknesses, e.g. incorrect setting-out of dialogue.

Independent writing activity

Give time for children to revise their writing. Those who have finished or written a very strong passage should continue, describing a third visit from Ernie in which Grandma pretends to be ill and Ernie is fooled into making her a reviving cup of tea.

Plenary

Listen to the new passages. Summarize what has been learned, referring to the Reminder Sheet.

Assessment

Pupils should be able to:
- punctuate and set out dialogue correctly
- reflect character through dialogue
- write short scenes that use dialogue effectively without resorting to a string of speech.

Model answers

Pupils' book 3 ☐ A

1 *Galoot* might mean a rather silly person.
2 He is big, tall (twice Joey's size), has narrow eyes, and sneers at Joey. He also seems to be easily taken in by Grandma.
3 He could be afraid of the shotgun, be worried about the mouse, have more deliveries to make.
4 She fabricates, would have been furious if there had been a dead mouse, never did things that cost a lot of money and was secretive about her business. Accept reasonable suggestions as to why she lies.
5 He *sneers* at Joey.

Pupils' book 3 ☐ B

6 *The kid's eyes widened. ...reaching around for the knob on the screen door behind him.*
7 e.g. *'Why, there's the post now.' He stood up and walked to the door.*
8 *'I found a dead mouse in your delivery yesterday.' The kid's eyes widened.*
9 e.g. *'This is Petronella,' he explained, picking up another crab. Without even a glance at me, Mr Staggers grabbed the bag of prawns and strode down to the boat.*

☐ 7A and 7B   Writing dialogue 🖪

Check correct punctuation, use of speech verbs and describing what is happening between what is said.

1 Correct the punctuation.

'hello, Mrs Patel', said Jason. 'How nice to see you again,' Said Mrs Patel. 'My Mum wants some apples, please, said jason', alright my dear', said Mrs Patel.

_____

_____

_____

2 Rewrite this dialogue, selecting more powerful verbs or using adverbs.

> *'Clear off,' said Sim.*
> *'What's up with you?' said Sam.*
> *'Just leave me be!' said Sim.*
> *'Keep your hair on,' said Sam.*

_____

_____

_____

_____

3 Rewrite the dialogue, adding descriptive text between what is said. Imagine what the speaker is doing. Imagine what the listener is doing. Is anything else going on? Look at the example.

> *'Watch out!' Dad yelled.*
> *'It's ok,' muttered Naomi.*

> *'Watch out!' Dad yelled, rushing to grab the dog's collar as it raced up the path.*
> *Naomi felt so sick that she hardly flinched. 'It's ok,' she muttered.*

_____

_____

_____

7B *Writing dialogue*

Is this good writing?

> *'Let's look at it,' Tom whispered.*
> *'I don't think so,' replied Uncle Sam.*
> *'But it's mine,' whined Tom.*
> *'Give that back,' shouted Uncle Sam.*

To improve it you can:

1   Describe what the speaker was doing, e.g.

> *'Let's look at it,' Tom whispered, peering at*
> *the golden ring that lay in his uncle's palm.*
> *'I don't think so,' replied Uncle Sam.*

2   Describe what the listener was doing.

> *'Let's look at it,' Tom whispered. Uncle Sam closed his fist tight and would*
> *not let Sam look any closer.*
> *'I don't think so,' he replied.*

3   Describe the listener's reactions.

> *'Let's look at it,' Tom whispered. With a shake of his head, Uncle Sam*
> *backed off.*
> *'I don't think so.'*

4   Add in other detail.

> *'Let's look at it,' Tom whispered. The ring glowed.*
> *'I don't think so,' replied Uncle Sam.*

Now rewrite the dialogue, adding your own ideas.

_____

_____

_____

_____

_____

_____

7 Writing dialogue

Set it out correctly

- Start a new line for a new speaker.
- Enclose what is said within the speech marks.
- End with a comma, question mark or exclamation mark – within the speech marks.

Bring it alive

- Use a powerful verb to show how the character feels, e.g. *he snarled*.
- Use an adverb, e.g. *said Sian angrily*.
- Balance the use of 'said', adverbs and powerful verbs.
- Have your characters say interesting things.
- Listen to what people say. Make a collection of odd sayings to use in your writing.

Avoid a string of speech

- Show what the character is feeling, e.g. *The kid's eyes widened*.
- Show what the speaker does. For instance, by using a comma and an 'ing' word to start the next part of the sentence, e.g.

  'Naw,' the kid said, reaching around for the knob on the screen door behind him.

Describe what the listener is doing

For example: *'Hi,' muttered Tom. His uncle stared at him.*

Describe the listener's reactions

For example: *'Look out!' yelled Sindi. Tim backed away, his mouth opening in horror.*

Add in other detail

For example: *'Look out!' yelled Sindi. The Zargreb began to tick.*

Verbs for character & action

The purpose of this unit is to deepen children's understanding of characterization, focusing on using verbs to show how characters feel. It links to the previous unit on dialogue, and work in Year 4 term 1.

NLS coverage

Key objective

SL **8** To revise and extend work on verbs (see Y4 objectives), focusing on:
- tenses: past, present, future
- forms: active, interrogative, imperative
- person: 1st, 2nd, 3rd.

Learned through

TL **Reading comprehension and writing composition**
1 To analyse the features of a good opening
3 To investigate how characters are presented, referring to the text, through dialogue, action and description
15 To write new scenes or characters into a story

Assessment criteria

SL By the end of this unit, pupils should be able to use verbs accurately and effectively, adapting them within a text for different effects.

TL **Writing composition**
Children should be able to write scenes for a story, using verbs to develop characterization.

Session 1

You will need OHT 8 and PCM 8A.

Shared reading

Display OHT 8, read through the passage and take initial reactions. Use the following to guide pupils:
- What sort of story is this? How do you know?
- What might happen next? Use the title as a clue.
- Which is the most exciting moment? How does the writer achieve this? Reread for clues.

Sentence level work

1 Reread the text, emphasizing the verbs so children can hear that most of the drama comes through the use of the verbs. Ask them to describe the action.

2 Focus on the opening. Alter it by changing verbs:
Before Lee could get to him, Tom himself began to edge down the mountainside. 'Lee! Help!' he warbled.
Compare with the original.

3 Ask pupils, in pairs, to quickly find powerful verbs that add excitement. List these as a class.

4 Ask pupils to find powerful verbs that suggest how the character is feeling or reacting. List these.

Independent activities

Direct pupils to PCM 8A where they are asked to rewrite a passage, altering the verbs to add excitement.

Plenary

Compare and contrast different ideas. Listen to how different verbs create different pictures of:
- what is happening
- the characters – how they feel and react.

Session 2

You will need pupils' book 3, Unit 8, pages 22–3, and PCM 8B.

Shared reading

1 Explain that this is the opening to a story by Morris Gleitzman, an Australian writer. Read the passage through. This can be enhanced if two good readers play the parts of Limpy and Uncle Bart, and the teacher is the narrator.

2 Discuss reactions – what makes this amusing? Which lines or words create humour?

3 Make two lists to note what we know about Limpy and Uncle Bart. Encourage the idea of searching within the text for clues.

Sentence level work

1 Take the opening few lines and simply identify the verbs. This should help children who are unsure about what makes a verb. (*said, hate, looked, smiled, stack, chuckled, are, felt, prickle, hopped*)

2 Collect any informal use of dialogue, e.g. *stack me*. Discuss how informal language is appropriate and useful in dialogue. List a few local expressions that might be handy to make dialogue sound realistic.

3 Discuss the idea of tense – past, present and future. Try transforming the opening into the present so that the action is happening 'now' (Jacqueline Wilson tends to write in the present), e.g.
'Uncle Bart,' says Limpy. 'Why do humans hate us?'
Uncle Bart looks down at Limpy and smiles fondly.

4 Discuss the impact on the reader of writing in the present tense. Does it make it more immediate? Discuss possible dangers, e.g. forgetting and slipping into past tense. This should be at the front of pupils' minds when they reread and revise their work.

Independent activities

Children complete questions A and B in the pupils' book. Question B asks pupils to transform another section from past to present tense as well as requiring them to focus on verb usage. Use PCM 8B as an extension activity.

Plenary

Use the plenary to listen to responses to question 10 in the pupils' book. Discuss the impact of writing in the present. Then listen to the results from the PCM. How successful have they been in staying in character – angry or shy – by using the appropriate verbs?

Session 3

You will need pupils' book 3, Unit 8, pages 22–3, and the Reminder Sheet.

Shared writing

The task is to continue the dialogue between Limpy and the grasshopper. Begin by rereading the passage. Make a list of ideas about what might happen next, leading up to the end of the chapter.

Write together

Select an idea for the rest of the chapter. Demonstrate the next paragraph, focusing on selecting verbs with care to show character; move the action forward.

Remind the class of what they learned about writing dialogue in Unit 7. Use the Reminder Sheets from both units.
Example: *'No it doesn't,' muttered Limpy, his eyes welling with tears. 'I loved Uncle Bart.' He gulped a few times and stared across the road.*
'Snap out of it, kiddo! You cane toads don't know nothing!' buzzed the grasshopper.

Independent writing activity

The children continue the story. Before writing they should decide on what will happen and share ideas in pairs. Remind them of their focus, using the Reminder Sheets from Units 7 and 8. More confident writers could try writing in the present.

Plenary

Listen to a few drafts. Ask the class to identify effective uses of verbs.

Session 4

You will need a section of work you have written, or one written by a pupil, on OHT, and the Reminder Sheet.

Shared writing

Remind pupils of the focus – continuing the story of Limpy, using verbs to reflect character. Ask the class to share their stories so far in pairs. As they read, they should underline in red any verbs that they think are especially powerful. Come together as a class and make a long list of these powerful verbs that show action or character. This bank can be used by the class to enhance their own writing.

Write together

Use the following passage as a way of focusing on revising to improve the choice of effective verbs. Draw ideas for improvements from the list of verbs.
The grasshopper leaped onto the high bank and looked down at Limpy. 'Come on, kiddo, get yourself up here,' he said. Limpy looked at his uncle for the last time and went up the bank.
'Where are we off to?' he said. The grasshopper went on ahead. Limpy came after him.

Independent writing activity

Everyone revises, focusing upon the quality of their word choice. They should draw on the class list where they have used bland verbs such as *look, went, came* or *got*. More confident pupils need to check for consistency in their use of the present tense.

Plenary

Listen to final versions, read aloud in pairs with one child taking the role of Limpy and the other taking the voice of the cheeky grasshopper.

Assessment

Pupils should be able to:
- identify weak verbs
- select more powerful verbs
- use verbs to shift the action forward and to suggest characterization
- continue a story with the characterization consistent.

Model answers

Pupils' book 3 ☐ **A**

1 The reader may wonder what sort of creature is talking, why they are hated, and why Limpy is an idiot. The author uses a direct question to draw the reader in and drops in information piece by piece to inform the reader.

2 Indignant – he felt it was unfair to call him an idiot and it made him think that it was not surprising that no other toad had ever asked the same question.

3 He calls Limpy an idiot and humiliates him, he laughs at Limpy, he says *'some of the dopey ideas you youngsters come up with'*, he puts Limpy down.

4 So no one can see who Uncle Bart is calling an idiot – he feels self-conscious.

5 He gets run over!

Pupils' book 3 ☐ **B**

6 *chuckled*

7 *came roaring, straightened, rumbled, drove, thundered.*

8 *trembled*

9 *chortled*

10 *He doesn't have to. While Uncle Bart is getting his mucus in a knot about how humans definitely don't hate cane toads, a truck comes roaring round the corner in a blaze of lights, straightens up, rumbles across the road straight at Uncle Bart and drives over him.*

☐ **8A and 8B** Verbs for character & action ⊞

Ensure use of powerful verbs to indicate how characters feel, e.g. Tim looked = *Tim glared.*

Rewrite this dull passage, altering the verbs to make it more exciting.

Tim looked at his friend. The tree was beginning to move now. Max was too far up. There was no way that he would be able to continue to go. The branch would give.

There was a resounding crack. The tree moved and Max called. He seemed to be in the air for a moment and then came down. But half way down he managed to get a branch and hold on. His fingers held for dear life. He got himself up. Just as he was about to get onto the safety of the branch, it gave. He went like a stone and arrived with a sickening thud.

Tim came over.

8B Verbs for character & action

Transform this passage by changing the verbs and any other words you wish. You can change what the characters say and do. Make Greg sound angry and Mitch sound shy.

> 'Don't you know anything?' growled Mitch. He glared at his friend. Greg looked back and swallowed.
> 'I just want to get to the town,' mumbled Greg. Mitch grabbed a cream bun and attacked it as if he had not eaten for weeks.
> 'Very tasty,' he snapped, swallowing twice. Greg struggled over to where Mitch sat chewing, his cheeks bulging.
> 'Mitch, I want a cream bun too,' he whispered. His friend obliged, thrusting out his hand and seizing another tasty cake.

_____

_____

_____

_____

_____

_____

_____

_____

_____

_____

8 ◁ Verbs for character & action

What is a verb?

A verb can be thought of as a 'doing' word (*he <u>ran</u>*) or a 'being' word (*he <u>is</u> big*).

Verb tenses

■ The past tense explains what has happened. It is used for most recounts. Many stories are written in the past tense, e.g. *Limpy <u>hopped</u> across the road.*

■ The present tense describes what is happening. This can make a story sound immediate. It may also help the reader to identify with what is happening, e.g. *Limpy <u>hops</u> across the road.*

■ You can create a future tense by using 'will', e.g. *Limpy <u>will cross</u> the road.*

Tightening verbs

Sometimes you can make your writing more dramatic by removing some parts of a verb. For example, which of the following two sentences is more powerful?

Limpy was hopping across the road or *Limpy hopped across the road.*

Often you can trim back the 'ing' and lose the extra verb 'was'.

Using powerful verbs

Powerful verbs are very precise. They tell the reader exactly what is happening. For example, which of the following two sentences is more precise?

The horse went down the lane or *The horse cantered down the lane.*

Powerful verbs can suggest what a character might be feeling. For example, which of the following two sentences tells us most about Limpy?

Limpy went his way across the highway.

or

Limpy slumped his way across the highway.

Powerful verbs can move the action forwards. For example:

The toad fell.

Whenever you use the following verbs, always pause and think whether you need a more powerful word:

went   came   look   ate   got   go   said

Make collections of other verbs that might be used in their place.

UNIT 9

Writing instructions

The purpose of this unit is for pupils to think about varying instructions depending on the audience, from formal to informal. It focuses upon using the imperative mood, and links to previous work this term on using verbs.

NLS coverage

Key objective

SL 9 To identify the imperative form in instructional writing and use this when writing instructions

Learned through

TL Writing composition
25 To write instructional texts, and test them out

Assessment criteria

SL By the end of this unit, pupils should be able to use the imperative form, varying the effect of this depending on the audience.

TL Writing composition
Children should be able to write a clear set of instructions, adapting the style according to audience and purpose.

Session 1

You will need OHT 9 and PCM 9A.

Shared reading

1 Display OHT 9 and read it through with the class. Who would this be useful for (audience)? What is its purpose? What type of text is this, and how did you know? Make a quick checklist of what the children know – this can be added to as you go along.

2 Discuss the meaning of the instructions.

3 Ask pupils, in pairs, to discuss the advice. If you had to remember just three points what would they be? Put the list in order of the most crucial points.

Sentence level work

1 Notice the use of the word 'you' in introductory sections. This helps to make it sound friendly, as if the writer is talking directly to the reader.

2 Underline the verbs in the list of bullet points. Where do they come in the sentence? Introduce children to the idea of the 'imperative', where the verb expresses a command.

3 Discuss why the sentences are written in the imperative (they need to be brief and clear – to tell people what they need to do – and memorable).

Independent activities

Direct pupils to PCM 9A in which they look at two sets of instructions. They are asked to decide which is more effective, and why. In pairs, they produce a set of advice about writing instructions.

Plenary

1 Listen to the advice sheets and create a whole-class checklist. This should cover:
   - the basic structure
     - a 'how to' title
     - a beginning section in which the reader is introduced to the instructions
     - a list of what is needed, e.g. tools and materials (in order)
     - what to do (in order)
     - an end section.
   - language features
     - commas in a list
     - colons
     - imperative form
     - verbs near the front of sentences
     - clear and simple sentences.

2 Take one example and show how the tone can be lightened by using the word 'you', e.g.
Plant the bulbs in Spring.
or
You should plant the bulbs in Spring.

Session 2

You will need pupils' book 3, Unit 9, pages 24–5, and PCM 9B.

Shared reading

1 Read the recipe through. Does it sound inviting? How does the writer manage this?

2 Discuss the audience and purpose.

Sentence level work

1 Which words or phrases suggest that this is not a 'formal' set of instructions, and that it is aimed at a young audience?

2 Check the instructions against the checklist to see what features are used and note any variations.

Independent activities

Children answer questions A and B in the pupils' book. The main challenge is to rewrite the final section, making it simpler to follow. (Direct a few children to put their rewrite onto a blank OHT for use in the plenary session.) PCM 9B acts as a prompt for children to create a set of instructions related to something that they know about.

Plenary

Listen to the rewriting of the recipe's final section. Use the pupil rewrites on OHT to see how much easier the instructions are (and to check for accuracy).

Session 3

You will need pupils' book 3, Unit 9, pages 24–5, and the Reminder Sheet.

Shared writing

The task is to write a recipe in a chatty style like Jamie Oliver. It should be aimed at young people and the content should be a favourite recipe. A good way to start is to list the key points, e.g. *boil egg, shell it, mash it up, add mayonnaise, make sandwich.*

Write together

Demonstrate how to turn the list into a recipe. Focus on making the tone friendly and modern, and ensure that the verbs are 'bossy' – imperative, e.g.

Feeling peckish? This is a recipe that I often use when my mates come round and we get the munchies. It's easy enough. I love it. If you want, you can lob in other bits and bobs. I like adding in slices of mushroom or a slice or two of tomato.

Serves 2.
A couple of eggs
A jar of mayonnaise
Butter for spreading
4 slices of bread plus all the usual things like knives, forks and so on.

Boil up the eggs. Leave them a while so that they get really hard…

Independent writing activity

The children write their own recipes.

Plenary

Listen to examples, highlighting where the writing sounds appropriately informal.

Session 4

You will need a section of work you have written, or one written by a pupil, on OHT, and the Reminder Sheet.

Shared writing

Remind pupils of the focus – writing a set of instructions in a friendly, informal style. You may wish to revisit the instructions written previously and then move on to the next challenge. This is to transform a set of instructions from a very formal, dull tone into something more informal, aimed at children in Year 5. Read the example below and discuss how it might be changed into sounding quite inviting.

To play 'tag'.
This is a good game to play in break-times.
What you need: an adult to supervise, two teams, an open space.
What you do:
Select one person as the 'tag'. This person must chase everyone else. This person tries to touch someone else. If someone else is touched then they become 'tag' as well. This is very exciting.

Write together

Model altering the opening, e.g.
Tag along?
Ever get bored at break-times? Yes, then learn how to play this amazing game and…

Independent writing activity

The children continue altering the instructions, trying to liven them up, and thinking about their audience and how to appeal to them.

Plenary

Reread the initial instructions and contrast this with the revised pieces. Discuss particular effects that have been used to appeal to the younger audience.

Assessment

Pupils should be able to:
- use the imperative mood appropriately
- write a well-structured set of instructions
- adapt instructions according to the audience.

Model answers

Pupils' book 3 ☐ A

1 Various answers possible – justification needed.
2 To make it seem modern and appealing to younger readers.
3 The first introduces the recipe. The second gives ingredients in a list. The third tells you how to make it and is in the imperative.
4 *scrumptious; nothing better; try throwing them…; kinda; Bloomin' gorgeous.*
5 Younger readers – the language is appealing to them as it is less formal than most recipes. It is rather like he is talking straight to the reader.

Pupils' book 3 ☐ B

6 Present.
7 Past – because you would have already cooked it.
8 *try throwing…; add the olive oil…; fry and…; crumble in the chilli…; toss over.*
9 This recipe for pan-toasted almonds does not take long to make. Serve with cold drinks or scatter on salads.
10 e.g.
- First add the olive oil and almonds to a hot frying pan.
- Now fry and gently toast the almonds until they are golden brown, shaking the pan at regular intervals so the nuts cook evenly.
- Then crumble in the chilli, according to taste, and add the sea salt.
- Finally mix it all together and serve hot on a large plate.

☐ 9A Writing instructions ⊡
The second set of instructions is obviously better – it is organized, clear, direct and yet friendly.

☐ 9B Writing instructions ⊡
Make sure that pupils select a topic for writing that interests them – and that they know about.

9A Writing instructions

Look at these two sets of instructions. Which is the most helpful, and why? In pairs, produce a set of advice about writing instructions aimed at someone who finds them hard to write.

Flying kites

You get a kite and throw it up in the air. You have to get a lot of wind. You need to be on a high place. It's great.

Learn how to fly high

HAVE YOU EVER WANTED to fly high? Well read these instructions and soon you will be able to fly your kite as high as you like.

You need: a good kite that is in working order, a high place such as a hill, a friend to help and plenty of wind (not too strong or your kite might blow away!).

What you have to do:

- Climb up a hill or any other such open, high place where the wind blows.
- Place the kite on the ground.
- Unwind some of the line.
- Get your friend to hold the kite up, facing so that the wind blows into the kite.
- Hold the end of the line and walk carefully backwards into the wind.
- As the wind fills the kite, ask your friend to let go.
- The kite should sail up.
- Steadily pay out the line as the kite rises.

It's easy enough – when you know how!

Ideas for topics to write instructions on

- Rules for a club, e.g. Pokemon, Gameboy, Nintendo, Playstation
- Instructions for collectors – of precious stones, stamps, bones, game cards, computer games
- Instructions on 'using' – getting a computer running, loading a computer game, skate boarding
- Instructions for 'playing' – playground games, team games, games with orcs and wizards
- Instructions on 'making' – a model machine, a secret hideout, a cool drink
- Crazy instructions – for a good party, a great school outing, a new teacher

How to make a totally new teacher

Fed up with your present model? Why not design and build your own? Follow these simple instructions and you can be the first kid on the block to have your own super automatic, customized teacher model! Don't delay.

What you need: basic teacher model, a good sense of humour, relaxed attitude, plenty of knowledge, calm manner.

What you do:
1. Take a sense of humour and add to the basic teacher model.
2. Leave to simmer for half an hour.
3. Stir in a pinch of relaxed attitude.
4. Spice up with a good knowledge of all subjects.
5. Leave to bake, covered with a topping of calm manner.

This teacher will make every year a special year!

9 *Writing instructions*

The basic layout

1 A title that explains to the reader what the instructions are about. Sometimes a catchy title is used to interest the reader.

2 An introductory paragraph that tempts the reader to use the instructions. It may also provide some handy hints.

3 What you need. This is a list of what will be needed, e.g. tools and materials. It is written in the order that the items appear in the instructions.

4 What you do. Again this is written in the order in which you need to do things. The sentences must be simple and clear so that the reader does not get muddled. Often the verb is near the front of the sentence and sounds rather bossy. This is called the 'imperative' form of the verb. It tells the reader what to do.

5 An end paragraph. This rounds the writing off. It may have some extra advice.

Remember

■ Think about the audience – adjust your style to suit who you are writing for.

■ Make the instructions clear for the reader or you will muddle them. When you revise your writing, pretend that you are the reader and know nothing. Ask yourself as you read – will the reader be able to follow these instructions?

■ Use diagrams and drawings if it helps to explain something complicated.

TERM 2

UNIT 10 *Creating different emphases*

The purpose of this unit is for pupils to begin to become skilled at manipulating sentences, reordering them to create different effects.

NLS coverage

Key objective

SL 1 To reorder simple sentences, noting the changes which are required in word order and verb forms and discussing the effects of changes

Learned through

TL Writing composition
11 To write own versions of legends, myths and fables, using structures and themes identified in reading

Assessment criteria

SL By the end of this unit, pupils should be able to reorder, and write, sentences to create different effects by using those parts of sentences that can be moved, for example: adverbs, prepositional phrases, subordinate clauses, similes, infinitives.

TL Writing composition
Children should be able to write incidents from a traditional tale, varying sentences for effect.

Session 1

You will need OHT 10 and PCM 10A.

Shared reading

1 Display OHT 10. Read the whole text through and take initial reactions.

2 Explore the following – Why do you think Jack needs three golden hairs? Why might the old woman be helping him? What might happen about the dream?

Sentence level work

1 Focus in turn on the top four sentences:
   a Which word could be moved to another part of the sentence? Try the word *cautiously* in different places. End by placing it at the front. Discuss the effect (it makes the sentence more dramatic, making the reader wonder why the boy is creeping cautiously). Demonstrate how, if you start with an adverb, you follow it with a comma. Then try moving *up the path* (prepositional phrase).

   b Which chunk can be moved? Demonstrate how *to complete the task* can be shifted to the front. Discuss the effect of moving the infinitive (*to complete*). Again, a comma is needed.

   c Which chunk can be moved? Explain that the subordinate clause can be moved to the front and a comma is needed.

   d Finally, the simile can move to the front, or the prepositional phrase *beneath the table* can move to after *hid*.

2 Reread the rest of the text looking for incidents where the writer has used – or could have used – reordering in any of the four ways mentioned, e.g. *Immediately, the giant awoke*.

Independent activities

Direct pupils to PCM 10A. The task is to rewrite each sentence, reordering to change the opening of the sentence.

Plenary

Go through each sentence, considering how it might be reordered. Discuss the effect of this on the meaning. (In the main, whatever you put first carries the weight of meaning.)

Session 2

You will need pupils' book 3, Unit 10, pages 26–7, and PCM 10B.

Shared reading

Read and discuss the Beowulf passage – Which is the most powerful image in the tale so far? Why is it easier to describe evil characters than good ones? What do you think will happen in this story? What do you think the theme of the story will be? (basic good over evil / defeating the monster)

Sentence level work

1 Take the first sentence and experiment with different ways of reordering. Discuss the different effects.

2 Reread and look for other sentences that might be reordered to good effect. Use the initial checklist to help, for example:
- adverbs
- prepositional phrases
- subordinate clauses
- similes
- infinitives.

3 Add on any new ideas, for example:
- 'ed' words (*Covered* in a green, horny skin…)

Independent activities

Children complete questions A and B in the pupils' book. Those who finish early should use PCM 10B to practise reordering.

Plenary

Use the plenary to listen to different ways in which sentences have been reordered. Discuss the different emphasis this gives the meaning. Add any new discoveries to the checklist, for example:
- 'ing' words (*Yelling*, he ran down the hill.)

Session 3

You will need pupils' book 3, Unit 10, pages 26–7, and the Reminder Sheet.

Shared writing

1 Reread the Beowulf passage to tune the children back into the text type. Revisit the checklist and different ways to vary the openings of sentences by moving pieces around. Remind children that this creates a slightly different emphasis.

2 Explain that the task is to write the next part of the tale in three scenes:
- Grendel awakes.
- He makes his way through the marsh towards the hall.
- He arrives at the hall.

Write together
Take the first scene and continue the tale. Refer to the checklist and try reordering sentences to strengthen the writing. For example:
First one eye, then another blinked slowly open. Grendel peered out through the marshes across the waste lands towards the forests. Was that the sound of singing and laughter? Tugging himself from his ancient lair, the great monster slithered easily out of the marsh like a great fish and waited for a moment, listening. Water dripped from his scaly body. His eyes gleamed green and red. In the distance he could hear the feast. He sniffed the air, smelling the scent of roasting meats. He was hungry from his sleep.

Independent writing activity

The children should take the three scenes and write them, a paragraph for each. Encourage them to try reordering sentences to gain different effects.

Plenary

Listen to, and comment on, different examples.

Session 4

You will need a section of work you have written, or one written by a pupil, on OHT, and the Reminder Sheet.

Shared writing

Remind pupils of the focus – reordering for effect. What can they recall from the previous session? Revisit the checklist.

Write together

Use different sentences from the children's writing. As a class, look at the chosen sentences and consider how they might be reordered to gain more impact. Refer back to the checklist.

Independent writing activity

Ask the class to revise any sentences that might be reordered for greater drama and impact. This is helped if, when marking, you have circled or put an asterisk by any sentences that would benefit from reordering.

Plenary

Listen to examples where sentences have been reordered and discuss whether this new order has improved the meaning.

Assessment

Pupils should be able to:
- reorder sentences to create a different emphasis
- use this in their writing to create dramatic effects
- write scenes from a traditional tale.

Model answers

Pupils' book 3 ☐ **A**

1 Generosity and strength.
2 It was majestic – the tallest, finest, grandest building ever seen.
3 Lived in the fens and marshes; beyond the forest; evil suited Grendel; half-man, half-fiend; supernatural strength; covered in green, horny skin; no sword could cut Grendel; came from a race of sea monsters, giants, goblins and other outcasts; sleeps for centuries.
4 Human laughter and music from the feast – the sound of people having fun.
5 He will hate it and attack the hall – because he is the opposite of happiness.
6 *Centuries ago, there lived a powerful warrior king; it was the tallest, finest building that had ever been seen in the land; in his kingdom; it was to be the feast to end all feasts; all this happened in distant times, etc.*

Pupils' book 3 ☐ **B**

7 Various possibilities – check for proper sentence construction, e.g. *In the fens and foul-smelling marshland beyond the forest, lived Grendel.*

☐ **10A** and **10B** **Creating different emphases**
ｐ

Various possible solutions – do make sure that the sentences are correctly punctuated, e.g. *While Jack tried to escape, the giant fell into a deep sleep.*

Rewrite these sentences, creating a different emphasis by reordering. Remember to use a comma.

Skinny Malinka sniggered meanly.

_____

The dog growled angrily.

_____

Digger ran crazily down the hill.

_____

Mrs Savage rushed past the empty classroom.

_____

Sinbad held on to the lamp because he was afraid of dropping it.

_____

The giant fell into a deep sleep while Jack tried to escape.

_____

The cat sat like a fat statue.

_____

The clouds drifted like gigantic whales.

_____

Sally ambled slowly down the path like an old woman because she was so tired.

_____

Susi flew easily through the air like an eagle while the King looked on in amazement.

_____

10B Creating different emphases

Rewrite this passage, reordering some sentences to make the writing more dramatic.

> Sam rose slowly from his bed. He crossed the room and looked out. It was early morning. He waited at the window while the carts trundled past. He stood there like a statue. Soon he would see his father again.
>
> Sam waited till midday came, to watch the guards changing over. He left the house covered in a cloak of invisibility. It was now or never. He began to run. But luck was not on his side. Sam tripped, racing across the lane.

Reordering sentences

Some parts of sentences can be moved around. This creates slightly different meanings and can help to vary the openings of your sentences. There are a number of different parts that can be moved. (Notice where the comma goes in each example.)

- **Adverbs**
  Slowly, Grendel rose from the marsh.

- **Prepositional phrases**
  At the end of the lane, Grendel waited.

- **Subordinate clauses**
  While the singing faded, Grendel paused.

- **Similes**
  Like a satellite, Grendel's eye blinked.

- **Infinitives**
  Grendel waited till night came, <u>to make sure</u> that no one saw him.

- **'ed' words**
  <u>Covered</u> in a green skin, Grendel lay waiting.

- **'ing' words**
  <u>Roaring</u> with pain, Grendel lay dying.

UNIT 11 Adapting a story poem

The purpose of this unit is to encourage pupils to think about how texts can be rewritten for different audiences and purposes. It links directly to thinking about different types of writing and their demands, which will be needed when pupils are tested on writing.

NLS coverage

Key objective

SL 3 To understand how writing can be adapted for different audiences and purposes, e.g. by changing vocabulary and sentence structures

Learned through

TL Writing composition

12 To use the structure of poems read to write extensions based on these

Assessment criteria

SL By the end of this unit, pupils should be able to discuss how writing might have to alter in order to change its text type, according to audience and purpose.

TL Writing composition

Children should be able to translate a simple scene from poetry into narrative, making the relevant adjustments.

Session 1

You will need OHT 11 and PCM 11A.

Shared reading

1 Display OHT 11, masking the narrative. Read and talk about the poem – What has happened? What is happening now?

2 Draw the sequence out as a simple storyboard showing the scenes. For example:
   - A ship passes the lighthouse and sees no light.
   - The ship brings the news back to the harbour.
   - They set sail.
   - In the night they see that the lighthouse is unlit.
   - Day breaks.

Sentence level work

1 Discuss what changes might need to be made to the poem to turn it into a story for children in Year 5. Make a quick list.

2 Translate the first verse into narrative, with help from the class. For example:

As we steered the great ship past the lighthouse we could not see any sign of life, let alone the light. All of us knew that three men lived on Flannan Isle and wondered what might have happened to them. We peered through the darkness, squinting at the dark shape, hoping to catch a glimpse of something that would tell us what had happened...

3 Now read through the bottom half of the OHT. Compare the storyboard sequence with the way this narrative is written, using a flashback (*We had heard that morning...*).

Independent activities

Direct pupils to PCM 11A. The task is to translate the poem into narrative, aimed at children in Year 5. Just before doing this, discuss and create a storyboard for the different scenes. Explain that each scene should be at least one paragraph.

Plenary

Listen to some of the narratives. Highlight effective writing, especially where ideas from previous lessons have been used, e.g. reordering, effective use of verbs.

Session 2

You will need pupils' book 3, Unit 11, pages 28–9, and PCM 11B.

Shared reading

1 Read through the poem 'Colonel Fazackerly'. Explain that it is the beginning to a longer poem and some verses are missing. (Ask some children to look for the poem after the lesson so that the class can hear the whole version. It is a popular poem and will be found in most classroom anthologies.)

2 Create a simple storyboard for the different scenes. For example:
   - The colonel settles down to have his drink.
   - The ghost appears.
   - The colonel talks to the ghost.
   - The ghost gives a cry.
   - The colonel invites the ghost to sit down.
   - The ghost tries to scare the colonel.

Sentence level work

1 Who might like this sort of poem? Discuss any likes or dislikes.

2 Talk through each verse, discussing any parts or words that puzzle the children.

3 Identify the poem's pattern.

Independent activities

Children complete questions A and B in the pupils' book. For extension work, use PCM 11B: Rewrite this verse as a paragraph.

Plenary

Use the plenary to run through answers to the questions.

Session 3

You will need pupils' book 3, Unit 11, pages 28–9, and the Reminder Sheet.

Shared writing

Explain that the task is to turn the poem, starting at verse two, into a narrative. Use the storyboard to help see the scenes clearly.

Write together

Give each scene a paragraph, for example:
As soon as the colonel had spoken, the ghost gave a tremendous scream. Shaking its arms, it proceeded to wander up and down the hall, howling and moaning. The colonel eyed it, whilst helping himself to another glass of sherry...

Independent writing activity

The task is to write the poem out as if it was a story for children in Year 5. Pupils should use the storyboard to help them see the different scenes. They should refer to the poem for words that might be useful in their writing. But it must sound like a story!

Plenary

Listen to several examples. Isolate any successful sentences that sound like a story and not just the poem copied out as prose!

Session 4

You will need a section of work you have written, or one written by a pupil, on OHT, and the Reminder Sheet.

Shared writing

Remind pupils of the focus – rewriting the poem as a story.

Write together

Review any particularly successful examples. Then use shared writing to continue the story. Begin by adding on to the storyboard and deciding the next few scenes, for example:
- The ghost tries to freeze the colonel.
- The colonel carries on drinking.
- The ghost gives up and shoots up the chimney.
- The colonel is left grinning.

For a moment the room was quite still. The colonel wondered what on earth might happen next. Really, he thought to himself, this was most amusing. At that moment the ghost struck. It floated down, covering the colonel with its coldest mist. The colonel shivered inwardly, but not once did he let it show. Instead, he undid his collar and muttered, 'Jolly warm for the time of year.'

Independent writing activity

The children continue the story, using the storyboard to help with planning, trying to keep the colonel in character and using techniques from previous sessions. They need to think about how to amuse or interest their audience.

Plenary

Listen to examples. Ask the class to identify especially effective sections of writing. Focus on those that 'sound like a story'.

Assessment

Pupils should be able to:
- explain how writing can be adapted for different audiences and purposes, e.g. by changing vocabulary and sentence structures
- adapt a story poem into a narrative
- use a storyboard for simple planning in scenes.

Model answers

Pupils' book 3 ☐ A

1 It says that ... *someone or other forgot to declare to Colonel Fazack that the spectre was there.*
2 *furious flash and a flare; shot ... and shivered* – powerful verbs, alliteration.
3 Frighten him – maybe scare him away.
4 Pretends he is not scared and has mistaken the ghost for someone going to a fancy dress party.
5 Builds up a picture of the colonel and shows that it is 'firm' in his eye – he is not scared in the slightest.
6 Glowing.
7 He is trying his hardest to scare the colonel.

Pupils' book 3 ☐ B

8 Four lines, in rhyming couplets.
10 Write straight across the page; make rhymes less obvious; add in more detail; vary the sentence lengths.
11 Colonel sits down to have a drink, ghost appears, colonel talks to ghost, ghost tries to scare colonel.

☐ 11A Adapting a story poem ⊡

You could model the opening, e.g. *The sun blazed down as Mr Jenkins lit the barbecue. His sons – Terry, Jason and Frank – stood watching. They...*

☐ 11B Adapting a story poem ⊡

A possible model might begin: *Mr Patel decided that a tree-house would be a good idea. He grabbed a branch and began to haul...*

Change these three verses into scenes from a story.

The summer sky was clear and bright,
With swallows diving through the blue,
And on the lawn the three boys stood,
While Dad lit up the barbecue.

The flames exploded with a roar;
Smoke billowed out across the town.
The barbecue was quite a sight.
But Mum looked on with quite a frown.

The firemen came with their hoses;
The flames soon died right away.
Dad wanted to light another.
But Mum had a few things to say.

_____

_____

_____

_____

_____

_____

_____

_____

_____

_____

Rewrite this verse as a paragraph.

Dad decided to build a treehouse.
He was up the tree in a flash.
He said that the view was fantastic.
Then shot right down with a crash.

_____

_____

_____

_____

_____

_____

_____

11 ⟩ *Adapting a story poem*

Adapting writing

Always think carefully about who you are writing for (the audience) and what you are trying to achieve (the purpose) as this will influence your writing.

Some audiences for your writing

You might write for:

- a younger class
- people at home
- an elderly relative
- a friend on holiday
- another class
- a class in another school (by e-mail).

Some purposes for your writing

You might write to:

- entertain – with a story, a play, a poem
- amuse – with a joke or a tale
- frighten – with a ghost story!
- record – by making notes
- inform – with a report full of information
- explain – how something works
- recount – what happened
- instruct – how to get things done
- put forward different views – so others can think about issues
- persuade – because you want to get people on your side
- evaluate – to think about how effective something is.

Structure and choice of words

Different sorts of writing for different audiences may mean thinking about how you:

- structure the writing
- select the words and sentences.

For instance, if you were writing a report about sharks for younger children, you would want to keep it clear, simple and yet still interesting. You might use many pictures and few words. You would keep the vocabulary simple or use a glossary to explain.

UNIT 12 · *Handling nouns & pronouns*

The purpose of this unit is to develop pupils' ability to use nouns precisely, e.g. *Rottweiler* rather than *dog*, and to avoid muddling the reader by ensuring that the use of pronouns is clear. It links to work on pronouns in Year 3.

NLS coverage

Key objective

SL 4 To revise from Y4: the different kinds of noun; the function of pronouns; agreement between nouns, pronouns and verbs.

SL 10 To ensure that, in using pronouns, it is clear to what or to whom they refer

Learned through

TL Writing composition
11 To write own versions of legends, myths and fables, using structures and themes identified in reading

Assessment criteria

SL By the end of this unit, pupils should be able to distinguish between different types of noun; identify pronouns; avoid over-repeating pronouns and confusing the reader; select precise nouns.

TL Writing composition
Children should be able to add further scenes to a traditional tale.

Session 1

You will need OHT 12 and PCM 12A.

Shared reading

1 Display OHT 12, covering the text and revealing it line by line. Read it at an even pace.

2 Discuss how the twist occurs at the end.

3 How could this be rewritten to avoid the confusion?

4 Would the story still be as intriguing?

Sentence level work

1 Explain you will be looking at nouns and pronouns.

2 Read OHT 12 and underline the nouns (words which denote something/someone – like a label).

3 Categorize them by type:
  ■ common noun – name given to non-specific things (e.g. *tree, boy, girl, bird, flower*)
  ■ proper noun – name for specific things, starting with a capital letter (e.g. *Tim, Woolworths, Oxford*)
  ■ collective noun – name for a group of things (e.g. *pack, flock, wood*).

4 Discuss and find:
  ■ singular noun – just one
  ■ plural noun – more than one.

5 Introduce the point that, when writing, it is helpful to be precise when choosing nouns. For example, which is the stronger sentence?
The man got into the car.
or
The BFG squeezed into a Skoda.

6 Now focus on pronouns – which stand in place of nouns, e.g. *her, she, them, it, me*.

7 Discuss the importance of being clear to what or whom the pronoun refers and warn pupils that they must be on their guard not to muddle the reader. This can be avoided by careful rereading as they write.

Independent activities

Direct pupils to PCM 12A – an activity divided into two parts. In the first passage they are asked to list the common nouns, proper nouns and collective nouns, and to find five plurals and five singular nouns. They are then asked to improve the second passage by balancing the use of nouns and pronouns.

Plenary

Go through the work. Summarize the types of noun and pronoun. Revisit the writing points – avoid a pronoun muddle by rereading, and use precise nouns.

Session 2

You will need pupils' book 3, Unit 12, pages 30–31, and PCM 12B.

Shared reading

1 Read the tale through. Which is the most memorable image?

2 Reread and listen for any good description, e.g. use of simile.

3 What might happen next?

4 Draw a storyboard or use a flowchart to show the sequence of events. For example:
   - Chulyen is hungry
   - sees a herd of whales
   - one eats him
   - he is in a dark cave
   - looks at the lamp
   - spirit girl appears
   - she warns him – don't touch the lamp.

Sentence level work

1 Quick recap: ask pupils to scan the passage and find a common noun, a proper noun, a singular noun, a plural noun, a collective noun, a pronoun.

2 Find the sentences with similes, and then imitate them to create new ones. For example:
   - The girl laughed, a laugh as clear as tumbling water. *The girl screamed, a scream as sharp as a thorn stabbing skin.*
   - A heart was beating like a great, slow, steady drum. *A dog was howling like a violent, gusting, reckless gale.*

Independent activities

Children complete questions A and B in the pupils' book. Most will be able to move on to PCM 12B which asks them to improve sentences by using precise nouns or a better balance of nouns/pronouns.

Plenary

Discuss the story again, relating it to other stories, e.g.
- Jonah – swallowed by a whale
- lamp stories
- Beauty and the Beast – which uses the idea of a rose that must not be touched.

Double-check the children's ability to identify nouns/pronouns and discuss the PCM sentences.

Session 3

You will need pupils' book 3, Unit 12, pages 30–31, and the Reminder Sheet.

Shared writing

Explain the task – continuing to write the tale, using the scenes listed in the pupils' book. Take each scene and brainstorm useful words, phrases, similes.

Write together

Demonstrate how to write up one scene as a paragraph, drawing on the brainstorming session, e.g.
For many days Chulyen the raven stayed in the darkness, listening to the dripping oil, watching the flame glow. His hunger grew until he could bear it no longer. So Chulyen dipped his claw into the oil and tasted it. It was thick and greasy. He could taste the ocean's swell and sweet fish. Mmmm. After that, whenever the girl's back was turned Chulyen dipped his curved claw into the pool of oil.

Independent writing activity

Remind children to reread as they write, avoiding any pronoun confusion. Then reread the story to pick up on the rhythm of the style. They write the next scenes, drawing on brainstormed ideas.

Plenary

Listen to scenes, identifying effective examples of style.

Session 4

You will need a section of work you have written, or one written by a pupil, on OHT, and the Reminder Sheet.

Shared writing

Remind pupils of the focus – writing the second half of the tale. Begin by reading or showing successful examples. Look at instances of confusion due to muddled use of pronouns.

Write together

Demonstrate how style can be improved by drawing on work done in previous units. For example:

- adding in several similes to create stronger pictures
- choosing powerful verbs and apt adjectives
- reordering some sentences to vary openings.

Focus on securing a well-defined ending. This should comment in some way on what has happened, perhaps referring back to the opening.

Independent writing activity

In pairs the children read and edit each other's writing. They should ensure that the ending is sufficiently well defined – even if this means adding an extra paragraph.

Plenary

Listen to specific sentences where improvements have been made. Caution against the temptation to overwrite – putting in too many adjectives, for instance.

Assessment

Pupils should be able to:

- identify different types of noun and pronoun
- avoid causing confusion when writing, using pronouns and nouns
- write scenes from a tale.

Model answers

Pupils' book 3 ☐ A

1 Whale (*Jonah*); lamp (*Aladdin*); beautiful girl (examples too numerous to mention!); speaking bird as main character; being told to leave the lamp alone (like the rose in *Beauty and the Beast*), etc.
2 *groaning ache of hunger; wrinkles of hunger; like a great, slow, steady drum*, etc.
3 He is magical, he is greedy, his hunger is never satisfied, he is silly.
4 Something will go wrong – it will go out, etc.

Pupils' book 3 ☐ B

5 Chulyen.
6 common nouns – *water, tails, meat, girl, fish*, etc; collective – *herd, school*; singular – *sea, half-light, cavern, heart, wick, oil*, etc; pronouns – *he, I, who, it, she*, etc; plural – *shadows, eyes, wings, waves, whales*, etc.

☐ 12A Handling nouns & pronouns ⏚

1 common nouns – *bird, fish, day, tree, field* etc; proper – *Chulyen, Chakka*; collective – *flock, forest*; plural – *fish, waves, sheep, flowers, roots, apples, puddles*; singular – *raven, bird, sea, tree, lamb*, etc.
2 *Mrs Assam gave Timmy a bike for his birthday. He rode it down the lane but it broke. He took it back to his Dad. His Dad told him to speak to his Mum about mending it.*

☐ 12B Handling nouns & pronouns ⏚

1 *Grimaldi crossed Oxford Street.*
2 *Mr Mancini spoke to Naseem about his behaviour.*
3 *Jessy climbed Mount Baldy.*
4 *The parrot sat in a fir tree.*
5 *The Mercedes drove into Birmingham and stopped outside Woolworths.*

1 *Tim generously gave Tom a car.*
2 *Because it was cold, Sim gave Sam a bicycle.*
3 *Sandi fell asleep because her Mum was working late at the factory, packing soap into coloured boxes. That always made her Mum smell of soap.*

12A Handling nouns & pronouns

1 Read the passage and identify the common nouns, proper nouns, collective nouns, five plural nouns and five singular nouns. (Either underline each type of noun in a different colour or make a list.)

> Chulyen the raven was a great bird. He lived by the sea eating fish. Every day he perched in a tree watching the waves. Nearby was a flock of sheep. Chulyen had never tasted lamb before and he was curious. He hid amongst the flowers at the edge of the field. He waited. But along came Chakka the coyote. He too felt hungry and the forest was empty. Chakka was fed up with eating roots, green apples and drinking from dirty puddles. He needed a good meal.

2 Improve this passage by changing a few nouns into pronouns.

> Mrs Assam gave Timmy a bike for his birthday. Timmy rode the bike down the lane but the bike broke. Timmy took the bike back to Timmy's Dad. Timmy's Dad told Timmy to speak to Timmy's Mum about mending Timmy's bike.

_____

_____

_____

_____

Handling nouns & pronouns

Improve these sentences by using precise nouns.

1. The man crossed the road.
2. The teacher spoke to the boy about his behaviour.
3. The girl climbed the mountain.
4. A bird sat in a tree.
5. The car drove into the town and stopped outside the shop.

_____

_____

_____

_____

_____

_____

_____

Rewrite these sentences, getting rid of the muddle.

1. Tim gave Tom a car. He was generous.
2. Sim gave Sam a bicycle. It was cold.
3. Mum was working late at the factory, packing soap into coloured boxes, so Sandi fell asleep. She smelled of soap.

_____

_____

_____

_____

_____

12 Handling nouns & pronouns

Nouns

Nouns are words that denote something or someone. They act like a label.
There are different types:

- common noun – a name given to non-specific things (*tree, boy, girl, bird, flower*)
- proper noun – a name for specific things, starting with a capital letter
  (*Tim, Woolworths, Oxford*)
- collective noun – a name for a group of things (*pack, flock, wood*)
- singular noun – just one (*dog*)
- plural noun – more than one (*dogs*).

When writing

It is often helpful to be precise when choosing nouns. For example:
  The BFG squeezed into a Skoda

rather than
  The man got into the car.

Try to avoid writing sentences in which the nouns do not create a strong picture for
the reader. For example:
  The man crossed the road.
  The bird sat in the tree.
  The girl got into the car.

Replace the common nouns with something more precise to bring the sentences
alive. For example:
  Lanky O'Neil crossed Princes Street.
  The vulture sat in the oak tree.
  Jenna got into the Mercedes.

Pronouns

Pronouns stand in the place of nouns, e.g. *her, she, them, it, me.*

When writing

Try not to muddle the reader. Be clear to what or whom the pronoun refers.
Muddles like this can be avoided by careful rereading and revising as you write.

UNIT 13 *Complex sentences*

The purpose of this unit is for pupils to develop the use of complex sentences in the context of writing a fable. It links to previous work on using commas to secure grammatical boundaries as well as writing traditional tales.

NLS coverage

Key objectives

SL 5 To use punctuation effectively to signpost meaning in longer and more complex sentences

SL 9 To secure the use of the comma in embedding clauses within sentences

Learned through

TL Writing composition
11 To write own versions of fables, using structures and themes identified in reading

Assessment criteria

SL By the end of this unit, pupils should be able to:
- use complex sentences to add in extra information and detail to a sentence
- punctuate a sentence where a subordinate clause has been embedded.

TL Writing composition
Children should be able to write a simple fable, leading to an appropriate ending.

Session 1

You will need OHT 13 and PCM 13A.

Shared reading

Display OHT 13, covering the top part to hide the odd six sentences. Read through the story, and discuss it with the class. What type of story is this? What are the main features of this sort of story? (Begin a checklist.) What is the main theme of the tale – how do we know?

Sentence level work

1 Now reveal the top six sentences and look at them one by one.

2 The first two are simple sentences – one clause.

3 The third is a compound sentence – it is like two simple sentences (clauses) joined by 'and'. Compound sentences are joined by 'and', 'but' or 'so'. It will help if you underline the two clauses.

4 The fourth is a complex sentence. Look carefully at it. It is the same as the first sentence but a chunk has been dropped into it (*who lived on the hill-side*). The main clause (can stand on its own, the most

important part) is *the hare was proud*. The subordinate clause (cannot stand alone, relies on the main clause, adds extra information) is *who lived on the hill-side*. Notice how commas are used. Make a quick list of other information that could be dropped in, e.g. *who was a fast runner, who laughed at the tortoise.*

5 The fifth is a complex sentence. Which is the main clause? (*the hare ran quickly*) It will help if you underline the two clauses in different colours. Put a box around the connective *while*. The connective comes before the subordinate clause.

6 The last is a complex sentence – though the connective (*though*) is at the start of the sentence, and so is the subordinate clause (*though she was slow*). Note that if a sentence starts with a subordinate clause, that clause is followed by a comma.

Independent activities

Direct pupils to PCM 13A which gives pupils the opportunity to practise making complex sentences.

Plenary

Reread the OHT and look at how the writer varies the sentences used – balancing simple, compound and complex. Check some answers to the PCM, listening to different ideas.

Session 2

You will need pupils' book 3, Unit 13, pages 32–3, and PCM 13B.

Shared reading

1 Who is the clever one?

2 Why do you think this?

3 Think of three words to describe Old Toad.

4 What does Red Fox mean when he speaks to Old Toad?

Sentence level work

1 Look at the sentence *It was raining when Red Fox heard the news.* Which is the main clause? Which is the subordinate clause?

2 How would it change the meaning if you swapped the clauses round?

3 Invent other subordinate clauses that could go with the main clause *it was raining*, using 'until', 'before', 'while'.

4 Find another example of a complex sentence.

Independent activities

Children complete questions A and B in the pupils' book. Use PCM 13B for those who are struggling.

Plenary

Use the plenary to highlight the features of a fable – draw up a checklist. Go through the questions about complex sentences. Focus on the idea that the main clause stands on its own, making sense on its own – and the subordinate clause is an extra piece tagged on.

Session 3

You will need pupils' book 3, Unit 13, pages 32–3, and the Reminder Sheet.

Shared writing

Reread the fable about Red Fox and Old Toad. Revisit the idea that writing needs a balance of sentences – simple for clarity, compound for flow, and complex to add in extra detail and information. Select an idea from the list of morals, e.g. *do not play with fire or you*

will singe your fur. Discuss a simple story line with the class and create a list of scenes. For example:

- A squirrel is lonely.
- It sees a lion sleeping.
- It makes friends.
- The lion says it is cold.
- Squirrel builds a fire.
- And nearly gets roasted up and eaten by the lion!

Write together

Remind the children that you want to vary your sentences, especially trying some complex sentences with a clause 'dropped in', or using a connective. (There is a useful list of connectives on the Reminder Sheet.) Refer back to the toad story and use the same sort of opening. For example:

Cleaning her fur one day, Young Squirrel decided that she was lonely. Why, she had hardly any friends in the great forest. So, after packing her belongings, Young Squirrel set off to find a friend.

Independent writing activity

The children complete the tale – referring to the list of scenes (to aid paragraphing) and the Reminder Sheet. They should try to balance the use of different types of sentence, attempting some complex sentences. Referring to the connectives on the Reminder Sheet will help with this.

Plenary

Ask everyone to underline any examples of complex sentences that they have used. Then listen to examples of their writing. Comment on what is effective.

Session 4

You will need a section of work you have written, or one written by a pupil, on OHT, and the Reminder Sheet.

Shared writing

Remind pupils of the focus – writing a fable, using some complex sentences.

Write together

Take some examples from the children's work where the sentences are varied effectively. Identify the use of complex sentences to add in extra detail. Take some examples where the sentences could be enhanced by adding a subordinate clause, and show how this might be inserted. For example:

Squirrel picked up lots of twigs for the fire
becomes
Squirrel, <u>who was weary by now</u>, picked up lots of twigs for the fire.

Independent writing activity

The children check and revise their writing, working in pairs. Reading the stories aloud is essential. Work should focus upon adding a few subordinate clauses to see if this can add extra depth to the writing.

Plenary

Ask several children to read out examples of where they have enhanced their sentences.

Model answers

Pupils' book 3 ☐ **A**

1 Old Toad – someone out to trick others; Red Fox – a wily, cunning character.
2 He went to get his paw cured. He could see that the toad was covered in warts so any medicine he had must not be working!
3 A moral is a saying that states how we should behave. *Do not go around telling others what to do when you have not sorted out your own problems.*
4 Fairly short; end with moral; feature animals; often a battle of wits, ending with one animal being defeated or looking silly.

Pupils' book 3 ☐ **B**

5 ...*<u>who was as clever as a barrel of monkeys</u>,* ...
6 *<u>Carefully packing his bags</u>... <u>Without worrying about getting wet</u>...*
7 *<u>He could see Old Toad</u>, <u>who was surrounded by the animals</u>, <u>queuing up to be cured</u>.* The main clause is *He could see Old Toad.*

☐ **13A and 13B** Complex sentences ☐

Various possible answers. Check for the use of commas where a clause is dropped into a sentence or where a sentence starts with a long subordinate clause.

Complex sentences

1   Use the following to practise making complex sentences. Remember to use commas!

Tom	who was getting soaked	was empty.
The toad	which tasted foul	stole a loaf of bread.
The lion	which was blazing by now	gazed at the plump chicken hungrily.
The medicine	where the toad lived	climbed out of the swimming pool.
The fire	who had slept all morning	cured nobody.
The village	who was hungry	had warmed them.

_____

_____

_____

_____

_____

_____

2   Write six complex sentences using this main clause: *The dog barked.*
Use these connectives: *because, while, before, although, after, whenever*
at the start of the sentence or in the middle. For example:

   The dog barked because a robber had crept up the path.
   or
   Because a robber had crept up the path, the dog barked.

_____

_____

_____

_____

_____

Complex sentences

Join the clauses to make a complex sentence. Underline the main clause.
(This is the one that makes sense on its own.)

Toad hopped up the path	in case she saw something frightening.
Lion yawned	because he had seen a tasty grasshopper.
Zebra looked at her stripes	as long as his energy lasted.
Crocodile snapped his mouth shut	whenever he thought about mathematics.
Snake hissed angrily	as if he was cross.
Eagle flew across the forest	before going out for the night.
Emu stuck her head in the sand	until she felt better.

_____

_____

_____

_____

_____

_____

_____

_____

13 Complex sentences

Using complex sentences

A complex sentence has a main clause and one or more subordinate clauses.

Here are some different ways to build a complex sentence.

- You can drop a subordinate clause into a main clause. For example:
  Phil, <u>who was good at football</u>, came last in the sack race.
- You can use a connective to add a subordinate clause after a main clause. For example:
  Phil came last in the sack race <u>because he was tired</u>.
- You can use a connective to add a subordinate clause at the start of the sentence. For example:
  <u>Because he was tired</u>, Phil came last in the sack race.

The main clause can stand on its own and is the most important piece of information.

The subordinate clause cannot stand on its own. It relies on the main clause and it adds on an extra piece of information.

Try using these connectives

After   although   as   as if   as long as   as though   because   before if   in case   once   since   than   that   though   till   until   unless when/whenever   where/wherever   whereas   while

Remember

Commas are used after a long subordinate clause that begins a sentence.

Writing tip

Vary your sentences. Use complex sentences to add in extra ideas, information and detail.

UNIT 14 *Varying sentences for interest*

The purpose of this unit is for pupils to develop the ability to vary sentences, especially their openings. This is particularly important for children who get stuck at level 3 because their sentences tend to all be constructed in the same way – simple and compound with little variation. It links to the previous units on sentences.

NLS coverage

Key objective

SL 8 To construct sentences in different ways, while retaining meaning

Learned through

TL Writing composition
11 To write own versions of legends, myths and fables, using structures and themes identified in reading

Assessment criteria

SL By the end of this unit, pupils should be able to vary sentences to create more interesting writing, especially by varying their openings.

Session 1

You will need OHT 14 and PCM 14A.

Shared reading

Display OHT 14, covering the list and concentrating on the story. Read each paragraph through and discuss them with the class – How does the prince feel? Who do you think he finds? What might happen next? Which are the well-chosen words or phrases?

Sentence level work

1 Now look at the list. Run through the different sentence types.

2 Reread the passage, identifying different types of sentence.

3 Discuss how the passage works because of the variation.

Independent activities

Direct pupils to PCM 14A which gives them the opportunity to imitate different types of sentence.

Plenary

Listen to examples. Reread the passage and discuss what the different types of sentence might be used for:

■ simple – for clarity and dramatic impact

■ compound – for the flow
■ complex – to add in detail
■ 'ing' starter (called a non-finite verb) – to emphasize the action
■ 'ed' starter (called a non-finite verb) – to emphasize the action
■ adverb starter – to emphasize how something happens
■ connective starter – to add in extra detail or information
■ 'but' sentence – to make a dramatic point forcefully
■ one word sentence – for dramatic punch.

Session 2

You will need pupils' book 3, Unit 14, pages 34–5, and PCM 14B.

Shared reading

Read the passage through. What do we know about Leo? What do we know about the giant? Why might the giant be in prison? What might Leo do, and what are your reasons?

Sentence level work

1 Identify the different scenes, e.g.
 ■ Leo finds the window
 ■ his brothers tell him about the giant.

2 Identify different types of sentence and discuss their effect.

3 Identify any stylistic effects, e.g. similes.

4 Identify any well-chosen words.

Independent activities

Children complete questions A and B in the pupils' book. Use PCM 14B to practise making a range of sentence types.

Plenary

Use the plenary to go over the basic questions and listen to answers to PCM 14B.

Session 3

You will need pupils' book 3, Unit 14, pages 34–5, and the Reminder Sheet.

Shared writing

Explain that the task is to continue the tale. In pairs, children should make a list of the scenes that will need to be written. This might lend itself to an opportunity for more extended writing.

Write together

Demonstrate how to use the Reminder Sheet to prompt varying sentences during writing. You could direct less confident writers to focus on just a few types. Take a scene per paragraph, beginning from the end of the section in the pupils' book. For example:

The giant was waiting for him. Leo peered into the darkness between the bars. Silently, the giant peered out. 'What do you want?' hissed his voice.

'A friend,' whispered Leo. Smiling to himself, the giant settled down to tell Leo about his life. For hours the two spoke, until darkness crept across the palace. So it was every day, the giant and Leo talking like old friends.

Independent writing activity

The children continue the tale, referring to the Reminder Sheet, trying to vary their sentences for effect. They should use the list of scenes to help structure their writing.

Plenary

Listen to examples read aloud. Comment on variations in sentences that contribute to powerful writing.

Session 4

You will need a section of work you have written, or one written by a pupil, on OHT, and the Reminder Sheet.

Shared writing

Remind pupils of the focus – varying sentences to create interest.

Write together

Use one or two examples from the children and focus on improving a few sentences to enhance a couple of paragraphs. Also focus upon making sure that there is a well-defined ending, including some reflective comment on the tale.

Independent writing activity

Ask the class to identify several paragraphs and, with a partner, rewrite them, varying a few selected sentences to create more powerful writing.

Plenary

Ask several children to read the original sentences and what they have now been turned into. Then hear the whole paragraph. Has it worked?

Assessment

Pupils should be able to:
- vary sentences to create different effects
- vary openings to sentences
- continue a traditional tale.

Model answers

Pupils' book 3 ☐ **A**

1 Maybe he was lonely, bored, or curious about what his brothers had told him.

2 To make the words rhythmical, to give them emphasis.

3 He might feel left out or lonely because they are not kind to him.

4 Possibly to draw attention to himself.

5 Maybe he felt sorry for the Giant as he might be lonely too.

Pupils' book 3 ☐ **B**

6 *It was a frightening sound. He didn't believe them. A wasp buzzed angrily through the bars. Leo ran off.*

7 *Looking through it...*

8 *But as he turned...* – to emphasize that there was something there; *But next day he went back...* – to suggest he didn't believe his brothers after all.

9 *... he came across a tiny, barred window.* The subordinate clauses tell the reader that it was one morning, he was exploring the castle, the window was set in the bottom of a wall.

☐ **14A** Varying sentences ⬜

These sorts of sentence need to be part of the children's writing repertoire.

☐ **14B** Varying sentences ⬜

Check for the use of commas.

14A Varying sentences

Here are some different ways to vary sentences. Invent your own sentences, imitating the basic pattern of the examples given.

1 A one word sentence

Run!

_____

2 A 'but' sentence

But they were too late.

_____

3 An adverb starter

Slowly, they opened the door.

_____

4 An 'ing' starter

Muttering to himself, the old man struggled up the stairs.

_____

5 An 'ed' starter

Stunned by the blow, the giant staggered.

_____

6 A connective starter

Although it was snowing, the prince rode on.

_____

7 A simple sentence

The prince cried.

_____

8 A compound sentence

The prince cried and the giant wept.

_____

9 A complex sentence

The prince cried while the giant slept.

_____

Varying sentences

1 Make three sentences starting with words from this collection:

whispering   yelling   screaming   running   fighting   struggling
wishing

For example: *Whispering to himself, the prince plodded on through the wintry woods.*

_____

_____

_____

2 Make three sentences starting with words from this collection:

saddened   blinded   startled   watched   rushed   pushed   doomed

For example: *Saddened by the giant's tale, the prince blinked back his tears.*

_____

_____

_____

3 Make three sentences starting with words from this collection:

slowly   quietly   cautiously   silently   bravely   foolishly
desperately

For example: *Slowly and menacingly, the witch got to her feet.*

_____

_____

_____

4 Make three complex sentences using words from this collection:

although   as   after   because   though

For example: *He opened the door although his heart was beating fit to burst.*

_____

_____

_____

The prince searched for the giant. He crossed the mountains. He walked through the forests. He rode on and on. He came to a large city. He rode into the city. He found a place to stay...

This is dull writing because all the sentences start in the same way. They are also all very similar – about the same length and type. Good writers vary their sentences for interest and to create different effects. Try using the following:

- A one word sentence – for dramatic impact
  Run!

- A 'but' sentence – to make a point forcefully
  But they were too late.

- An adverb starter – to draw attention to 'how' something happens (good for building tension)
  Slowly, they opened the door.

- An 'ing' starter – puts the action first
  Muttering to himself, the old man struggled up the stairs.

- An 'ed' starter – puts the action first
  Stunned by the blow, the giant staggered.

- A connective starter – to add in more detail, information, explanation
  Although it was snowing, the prince rode on.

- A simple sentence – for clarity
  The prince cried.

- A compound sentence – for flow and easy reading, to help the story jog along
  The prince cried and the giant wept.

- A complex sentence – to add in more detail, information, explanation
  While the giant was sleeping, the prince cried.

UNIT 15 — *Varying sentence types*

The purpose of this unit is for pupils to enhance their writing by using different types of sentence. Begin to think about using some structures from oral storytelling in writing traditional tales. It links with previous units on sentence variation.

NLS coverage

Key objectives

SL 6 To be aware of the differences between spoken and written language

SL 8 To construct sentences in different ways, while retaining meaning

Learned through

TL Writing composition

11 To write own versions of legends, myths and fables, using structures and themes identified in reading

Assessment criteria

SL By the end of this unit, pupils should be:
- aware of the differences between spoken and written language
- able to use a variety of sentence types to create different effects.

TL Writing composition

Children should be able to vary sentences when writing a traditional tale.

Session 1

You will need OHT 15 and PCM 15A.

Shared reading

Display OHT 15, covering the four sentences at the bottom. Read the tale through. Has anyone heard this story before – what happens? If not – can anyone guess? Does this remind you of any other stories?

Sentence level work

1 Reread the tale and identify which sentences make this sound more like a 'told' story than a written one.

2 Look at the four sentences at the bottom of the OHT. Identify where these patterns are used in the story. What effect do they have?

Independent activities

Direct pupils to PCM 15A in which they are asked to use different sentence types to finish the tale.

Plenary

Reread the OHT and then listen to examples of the final two paragraphs, drawing attention to judicious and effective use of different sentence types.

Session 2

You will need pupils' book 3, Unit 15, pages 36–7, and PCM 15B.

Shared reading

1 What is going to happen?

2 How do the farmer and his wife differ?

3 What is the farmer's main strength?

4 What is the wife's weakness?

5 Why do you think the story is called 'Fish in the Forest'?

Sentence level work

1 Read through the passage and identify:
- 'and' or 'but' sentences
- the use of questions
- the use of exclamations
- sentences that sound more like speech.

2 Discuss the effect of these sentences. For example, questions draw readers directly into thinking about the points that the writer wants them to consider, they involve the reader and draw them into the story.

Independent activities

Children complete questions A and B in the pupils' book. Use PCM 15B to transform a written passage into a passage that sounds more like an oral retelling.

Plenary

Use the plenary to hear some of the rewritten passages.

Session 3

You will need pupils' book 3, Unit 15, pages 36–7, and the Reminder Sheet.

Shared writing

Reread 'Fish in the Forest'. Explain that the task is to continue the tale, using different sentence types and drawing to a well-defined conclusion.

Write together

1 List possible scenes to aid planning, for example:
   a The wife sees the treasure
   b She tells everyone
   c The king hears
   d He sends for the farmer
   e The farmer gets an idea
   f He hangs old fish on the trees
   g The farmer and his wife are taken to the king
   h The king demands to know about the treasure
   i The farmer's wife says it is under the kitchen floor
   j The farmer asks her what is growing in the wood
   k She says, truthfully, that the trees are full of fish
   l The king thinks she is mad
   m The farmer and wife go home!

2 Take the final two scenes. Recount what happens before you start writing. Then model writing a well-defined ending, using a variety of sentences. For example:
   The king stared at the farmer's wife in amazement. He swallowed. Had he heard correctly? Did she really think that fish grew on trees? Dotty! She had to be completely mad. Ah well, he thought to himself as he waved the pair away.
   So it was that the farmer and his wife made their way home. The farmer had managed to keep his secret safe beneath the floor, and every now and then he would raid the box for some cash. And the wife, she was happy to believe that fish grew in the forest, gold coins were under the ground and all was well with the world.

Independent writing activity

The children, in pairs, use the list of scenes to tell their own versions before writing the rest of the story.

Plenary

Listen to examples and draw attention to effective use of different sentence types.

Session 4

You will need a section of work you have written, or one written by a pupil, on OHT, and the Reminder Sheet.

Shared writing

Remind pupils of the focus – completing the tale and using sentence variation.

Write together

Focus on the following ending. Rewrite it, varying the sentences and improving the words as necessary to make it more effective.
The farmer and his wife went home. They walked through the forest. The stale fishes hung from the trees. The farmer smiled. The wife asked him to show her the treasure. She promised to keep it a secret in the future.

Independent writing activity

The children work in pairs to revise their end three paragraphs.

Plenary

Listen to a few examples, drawing attention to effective use of sentence variation. Discuss how 'and' sentences are often used at the end of a story.

Assessment

Pupils should be able to:
• use different types of sentence to add variation
• complete a tale, writing a well-defined ending.

Model answers

Pupils' book 3 ☐ A

1 Characters – clever farmer, daft wife, greedy king, curious villagers; setting – village, market, field; objects – eggs, turnips, rusty chest, hoard of gold, moonlight; events – she can't keep a secret, travelling to market, news reaching the king, digging turnips, finding gold, king might want the gold, burying treasure, digging at night; language – *Once upon a time, Can you keep a secret?, And if it was a thing worth knowing…* etc.

2 By emphasizing the question 'Can you keep a secret?' The word 'secret' is used three times at the start of the story, leading the reader to think that the tale is about what happens if you cannot.

3 He gets to know everything, he listens to gossip, he is greedy. Possibly shown like this because poor people were ruled, and taxed, by the rich.

Pupils' book 3 ☐ B

4 *'Well, one day the farmer was…'*, etc.

5 *Now, the farmer's wife could not keep a secret!* To emphasize how odd this might be – as it is crucial for the story.

6 To involve the reader in the story and emphasize that this is what the story is about.

7 Six sentences begin with 'and'. It makes it sound like a traditional tale that is being told.

☐ 15A   Varying sentence types ⌐⌐

Example: *Once the fisherman reached home he asked everyone what he should wish for. His wife wanted a baby. His blind mother wanted her sight back and his old father suggested that gold was what they needed most. Unfortunately, the fisherman had only one wish. What should he do? All evening he paced up and down thinking about the problem.*
Well, it was midnight when he suddenly had an idea. Yes! That was it! Without telling anyone what he was doing, he rushed down to the sea. He stood on the sand beneath the silvery moon and called out, 'Oh King of the fishes, I wish for my mother to see our baby in a cradle of gold!'
And so it was that the fisherman and his family were all granted one wish.

☐ 15B   Varying sentence types ⌐⌐

Example: *The wife stood in the kitchen. 'What on earth is that for?' she asked, as she stared where the farmer had been digging. Gold gleamed in an open box! Well, her husband was standing right by the gold, holding a spade. And he had been digging. So she began thinking about this and soon she realized that they were going to be rich. Money at last!*

Varying sentence types

Write the end of the tale using the list of scenes. Remember to use different sentence types, for example:

- questions
- exclamations
- 'and' sentences
- sentences that sound like speech.

The scenes

1. He gets home
2. His wife wants a baby
3. His mother wants eyesight
4. His father suggests money
5. He doesn't know what to ask for as he only has one wish
6. He goes back to the sea
7. He has an idea
8. He asks the fish 'for my mother to see our baby in a cradle of gold'

_____

_____

_____

_____

_____

_____

_____

_____

_____

_____

_____

_____

Rewrite the paragraph below, trying to improve the writing. Use one of each of the following sentence types to help, as well as making other changes:

- an 'and' or 'but' sentence
- a question
- an exclamation
- a few sentences that sound more like speech.

The wife stood in the kitchen. She looked at the hole that the farmer had been digging. There was the box of gold. Her husband was standing near the gold, holding a spade. He had been digging. She thought to herself that it was an amazing find. They would be rich.

_____

_____

_____

_____

_____

_____

_____

_____

_____

_____

_____

_____

_____

_____

15 Varying sentence types

There are many different ways to vary your sentences. If your sentences all sound the same, you run the risk of being boring. Here are four ways to vary them.

- **Use an 'and' sentence**
  Many writers use a sentence that starts with 'and' right near the end of their tale. This is taken straight from the tradition of storytelling. Strictly speaking, you are breaking a rule when you do this. So save it for the end of a story.
  For example:
  And so they made their way home.

- **Use questions**
  Questions involve readers in the story, drawing them in and encouraging them to think about the points you want them to consider. They can arouse readers' curiosity, making them want to read on to see what will happen.
  For example:
  What was making that noise?

- **Use a few exclamations**
  Exclamations are effective at dramatic moments or when you want to make a point forcefully.
  For example:
  Run for it!

- **Use some sentences that sound more like speech**
  This works especially well in traditional tales. It can help to make your writing talk directly to the reader in an open, friendly manner.
  For example:
  Well, as you can imagine, it was not a very pretty sight.

UNIT 16 Linking ideas in sentences

The purpose of this unit is for pupils to develop the ability to combine sentences to provide flow when writing a non-chronological report. It links all this term's work on manipulating sentences and is crucial in moving children from level 3 to level 4.

NLS coverage

Key objective

SL 8 To construct sentences in different ways, while retaining meaning through combining two or more sentences

Learned through

TL Writing composition
21 To convert personal notes into notes for others to read
22 To plan, compose, edit and refine short non-chronological reports, using reading as a source, focusing on clarity, conciseness, and impersonal style

Assessment criteria

SL By the end of this unit, pupils should be able to combine sentences in a variety of ways.

TL Writing composition
Children should be able to write a simple report using a set of notes.

Session 1

You will need OHT 16, PCM 16A, and the Reminder Sheet.

Shared reading

Display OHT 16, covering the bottom two paragraphs. Read down to *The river flows into the sea*, and take first reactions. Did this grab your interest? Is it well written? What do you notice about the way it is written? What advice would we give this writer?

Sentence level work

1 Now uncover the paragraph that starts *When rain falls...* Identify how the sentences are joined or linked. Make a list of words that help to link ideas, e.g. *when, or, to, which, as, eventually.*

2 Now reveal the bottom paragraph. Use the board or space on the OHT to rewrite the text, linking ideas and sentences together so that the writing sounds less staccato. For example:
As the rivers flow over the land, they cut into it, creating valleys and gorges. The sediment, eroded from the river bed, is swept along by the water.

Independent activities

Direct pupils to PCM 16A which gives them the opportunity to practise joining two sentences together. The Reminder Sheet has a list of helpful connectives.

Plenary

Run through the PCM, considering how effectively and logically the sentences have been combined.

Session 2

You will need pupils' book 3, Unit 16, pages 38–9, and PCM 16B.

Shared reading

1 Who might have written this passage about the Moon?

2 Who might read it and why?

3 What new facts did you learn?

4 If the writer had used more sub-headings, what might each paragraph have had as a heading?

Sentence level work

1 Make a list of points which apply to this style of writing – impersonal, present tense, scientific vocabulary, use of pictures to illustrate ideas, etc.

2 Read through the passage and identify the different connectives. Keep these for future reference.

3 Take the second paragraph and rewrite it as notes that the author might have used.

4 Take the note *Craters cover the surface of the Moon. Early astronomers thought the dark areas were oceans.* As a class, find ways to link these ideas, without resorting to 'and'. For example:
Early astronomers thought that the dark areas that cover the surface of the Moon were oceans. However, they were craters.

Independent activities

Children complete questions A and B in the pupils' book, which focus on thinking about the structure of the text as well as combining ideas. Use PCM 16B. This asks children to take some notes and turn them into a paragraph, making sure that some of the ideas are linked together.

Plenary

Use the plenary to focus on whether the ideas are well linked together. Is there a good balance between simple, clear sentences and the linking of ideas?

Session 3

You will need pupils' book 3, Unit 16, pages 38–9, and the Reminder Sheet.

Shared writing

Revisit the example text about the Moon. Explain that the task is to write something similar about the Sun. Some facts are given in the pupils' book to help.

Write together

Brainstorm other facts that the children know about the Sun. Use a series of boxes to group the information, and add in the information from the pupils' book. Boxes could be labelled:
Introduction – what is the Sun?
What is it like?
What does it do?
Other facts
End comment

Demonstrate how to cluster the information. Then take one cluster and turn it into a paragraph, reminding the children that it has to be impersonal, scientific, present tense and that they should link ideas where sensible. It can help to reread the Moon passage again to get the 'feel' of the style.

Independent writing activity

The children write the whole report, using the planning 'boxes' of information. Remind them to link ideas and use the Reminder Sheet.

Plenary

Children read their work aloud. Others listen for effective paragraphs that 'sound' as if they came from an encyclopedia.

Session 4

You will need a section of work you have written, or one written by a pupil, on OHT, and the Reminder Sheet.

Shared writing

Remind pupils of the focus – linking ideas within a passage on the Sun.

Write together

Look at examples that are successful and focus on several where stronger links might be made. As a whole class, improve a few sentences.

Independent writing activity

Where writing needs improving they should work on this in pairs. Anyone whose writing has been successful could write a brief passage on a topic that they know about, e.g. sharks, horses, pets, etc. They should use a few boxes to plan.

Plenary

Listen to improvements plus any new pieces of writing.

Assessment

Pupils should be able to:
• join sentences and link ideas
• write a simple, ordered report from notes.

Model answers

Pupils' book 3 ▱ A

1 Purpose – to serve as an introduction and define what the Moon is. It may be in bold to draw the reader's eye to where to start. Other bold words may be in a glossary, have entries elsewhere in the book or be key words.

2 Quarter size of Earth; made of rock; covered in craters, some over 100km across; made by meteorites.

3 *Because*

4 Phases of the Moon

Pupils' book 3 ▱ B

5 Not really – the conjunction 'but' needs something before it. However, many people write like this for emphasis.

6 *When giant lumps of rock called **meteorites** crashed into the Moon, the craters were made.*

7 *It is made of rock, and its surface is covered with huge round depressions, called craters, many of which are over 100 kilometres across.*

8 *Craters, which look like dark areas that early astronomers thought were oceans, cover the surface of the Moon.*

▱ 16A   Linking ideas in sentences ⏸

Examples:

1 *When the sun shines, it gets hot.*

2 *The wind blows so trees move.*

3 *In the desert nothing grows for it is too hot.*

4 *After the rain has fallen, it is wet.*

5 *Cars do not work when they run out of petrol.*

6 *The sun burns skin but it helps plants to grow.*

▱ 16B   Linking ideas in sentences ⏸

Various possible responses. Ensure good use of connectives to link different points, e.g. *65 million years ago, dinosaurs roamed the earth.*

16A Linking ideas in sentences

Join the two sentences together. There may be more than one way, but the sentences must make sense. The Reminder Sheet has a list of helpful connectives.

1 The sun shines. It gets hot.

_____

_____

2 The wind blows. Trees move.

_____

_____

3 In the desert nothing grows. It is too hot.

_____

_____

4 The rain has fallen. It is wet.

_____

_____

5 Cars do not work. They run out of petrol.

_____

_____

6 The sun burns skin. It helps plants to grow.

_____

_____

16B Linking ideas in sentences P

Turn these notes into a paragraph. Make sure you link some of the ideas together.

Dinosaurs

- dinosaur means 'terrible lizard'
- prehistoric reptile
- roamed earth
- 65 million yrs ago
- longest 27 m
- Tyrannosaurus Rex – 2 storey building
- smallest 27 cm – chicken size
- hundreds discovered
- fossilized bones
- mystery – died out

_____

_____

_____

_____

_____

_____

_____

_____

_____

_____

_____

_____

_____

_____

Linking ideas in sentences

Read the following:

> *In the winter animals hibernate. It is cold. They sleep till Spring.*
> *They wake up. It is warmer.*

Not very well written, is it? The ideas need to be linked together, for example:

> *In the winter, when it is cold, animals hibernate. They sleep until Spring*
> *when they wake up because it is warmer.*

Writing tip

When you are writing you will often need to link ideas together.
Connectives can be used to help make links. These are some of the most common:

after	*since*
although	*than*
as	*that*
as if	*though*
as long as	*till*
as though	*until*
because	*unless*
before	*when/whenever*
if	*where/wherever*
in case	*whereas*
once	*while*

UNIT 17 — *Bringing legends alive*

The purpose of this unit is for pupils to consider the difference between speech and writing. It focuses upon story telling and story writing.

NLS coverage

Key objective

SL 6 To be aware of the differences between spoken and written language, including:
- conventions to guide the reader
- the need for writing to make sense away from the immediate context
- the use of punctuation to replace intonation, pauses, gestures
- the use of complete sentences

Learned through

TL Reading comprehension and writing composition
3 To explore similarities and differences between oral and written story telling
11 To write own versions of legends

Assessment criteria

SL By the end of this unit, pupils should be able to discuss the differences between writing and speech.

TL Writing composition
Children should be able to retell a legend using some oral techniques that are suited to the written form.

Session 1

You will need OHT 17 and PCM 17A.

Shared reading

1 Display OHT 17 and read through the text. Take reactions.

2 Explain that legends are like traditional tales – but with a basis in some historical truth.

3 What do the children notice about the way it is written?

Sentence level work

1 Go through the text making a list of the features that make it sound like a transcript of speech rather than a written tale. For example:
- direct reference to audience (*well, I guess many of you...*)
- informal patterns (*... some I guess are true...*)
- use of questions to audience (*... I guess many of you have heard about Davy Crockett?*)
- reference to audience reaction (*... I can see some heads nodding...*)
- repetition of 'and', 'well' and 'you see'
- repetition for effect (*Well, there are some pretty good legends about Davy Crockett and some I guess are true and some I guess are not so true, but this story I'm about to tell you is as true as I sit before you...*)
- many compound sentences
- writing doesn't make sense away from the action (*he comes along like this... and he goes up the tree like this... And he looks out like this...*). In fact the ending does not work without acting out the actions. (As writing, this is the only part that does not work.)

2 As a class, try to rewrite the last part, filling in the actions.

Independent activities

Direct pupils to PCM 17A in which pupils are asked to use the flow chart to prepare a retelling of Little Red Riding Hood. This should be carried out in pairs, taking it in turns to tell the next scene.

Plenary

Listen to several examples. Take one scene and translate it into writing, filling any spaces, refining any 'ums' and 'ers', etc. Note that gesture, intonation and pauses are hard to write down.

Session 2

You will need pupils' book 3, Unit 17, pages 40–41, and PCM 17B.

Shared reading

1 Read the story of the Pied Piper 'Brightman'.
2 Does this differ from the version anyone knows?
3 Who did whom a favour?
4 Who was wrong?

Sentence level work

1 Form a large story circle and retell the story, taking it in turns to tell the next part.
2 As a class, begin a flow chart showing the first few scenes – no more, as this is the independent task.

Independent activities

Children complete questions A and B in the pupils' book. Use PCM 17B as a flow chart frame to write down the key scenes. For example:
- Brightman arrives
- He sees rats everywhere
- He promises to get rid of them
- He pipes them out
- They go into the river
- The townsfolk won't pay him
- He appears as a hunter
- He pipes the children out
- The town is left empty

Plenary

Use the plenary to discuss the key scenes. Also, talk about the facts given in pupils' book section B and whether the legend arose to explain away the truth. The evidence suggests:
- they might have been killed in a plague
- they might have joined the children's crusade
- they might have left to resettle in the East.

Session 3

You will need pupils' book 3, Unit 17, pages 40–41, and the Reminder Sheet.

Shared writing

Introduce the task – to prepare a retelling of the legend based on the notes / flow chart from the previous session. Explain that some embellishment is to be encouraged, though they must stick to the basic structure of the tale.

Write together

To help the children with their retelling, use a flow chart as a prompt and demonstrate a retelling.

Independent writing activity

In pairs, children work on a retelling. They should take it in turns to tell the next scene. Once they have told it twice over, then put them into fours. The pairs take it in turns to tell their own version to the other pair. Stop them and discuss how each retelling is a chance to refine and improve the retelling. It can act as a form of oral revising. Then move to a circle of eight. After this, each circle should vote on the best retelling within their circle.

Plenary

The 'winning' pairs retell for a final time to the whole class. Discuss what they should do to achieve a good retelling. For example:
- speak clearly
- look at the audience
- don't rush
- vary the volume, expression and pace
- use expression
- know the tale well
- add in new bits but keep to the structure
- use language well.

Session 4

This session moves the retelling into writing.

Shared writing

Revisit the features of a good retelling.

Write together

Ask the strongest pair to retell their opening. Translate this into writing.

Independent writing activity

The children retell their tale in their heads, scene by scene, and write it down. They can use some oral techniques but must make sure that the tale works as writing – where gesture, etc, cannot be seen.

Plenary

Listen and comment on some of the retellings.

Model answers

Pupils' book 3 ☐ **A**

1 It names a specific place, gives a date, says the man *was allegedly called Brightman*, names a river and provides the actual day and time – all these make it sound as if it might have happened.
2 They refused to pay the piper.
3 Maybe they were poor or they thought that they could get away with not paying.
4 The piper was *terrifying*; and they didn't realize the children would all disappear.

Pupils' book 3 ☐ **B**

5 The notes need to be simple, e.g. *Hamelin overrun by rats – Piper agrees to get rid of them – he pipes and drowns rats – townspeople won't pay – he pipes children away.*
6 The evidence suggests that the children may have died in a plague, left on the children's crusade or been moved East. Maybe the townspeople made up the story to cover their grief or to hide something that they had done.

☐ **17A** and **17B**   Bringing legends alive 🔁

Encourage the children to retell their tale in pairs and then in fours. The retelling will give them a chance to orally redraft and refine their tale.

Use the flow chart below to prepare a retelling of Little Red Riding Hood.

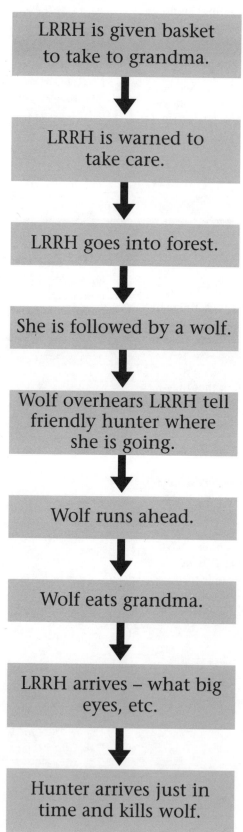

LRRH is given basket
to take to grandma.

↓

LRRH is warned to
take care.

↓

LRRH goes into forest.

↓

She is followed by a wolf.

↓

Wolf overhears LRRH tell
friendly hunter where
she is going.

↓

Wolf runs ahead.

↓

Wolf eats grandma.

↓

LRRH arrives – what big
eyes, etc.

↓

Hunter arrives just in
time and kills wolf.

Use this flow chart frame to write down the key scenes of the story.

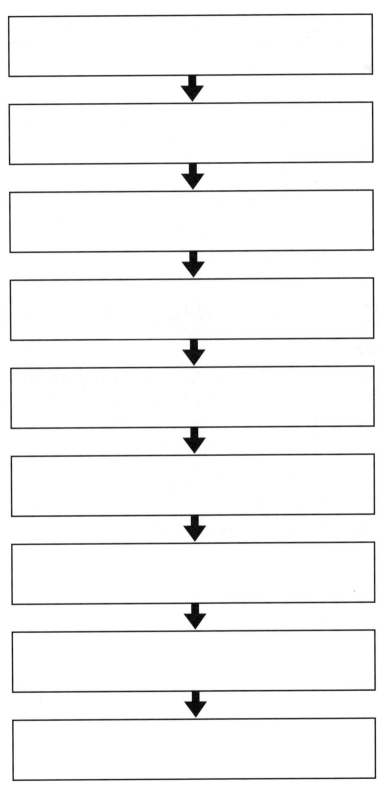

17 *Bringing legends alive*

Telling stories

Telling stories can be great fun. But you have to prepare well.

- Turn the story into bare bones so that you know the basic pattern.
- Practise telling the tale.
- Speak clearly.
- Look at the audience. Look into their eyes as you tell the tale.
- Do not move about too much.
- Use expression.
- Vary the volume – loud and soft.
- Use pauses to create dramatic tension.
- Vary the pace – quick and slow.
- Use language well.
- Add in new bits with each retelling, but keep to the structure.

Writing stories

Telling a story can help your writing. Telling before writing can help you improve the story and find out how it should be told. But writing is not the same as telling.

- Watch out for too many 'and's!
- Make sure that you use words to replace gestures, expressions on your face or actions that you make when telling.
- **Remember** – the reader cannot see or hear you!

TERM 3

UNIT 18 *Investigating clauses*

The purpose of this unit is to identify clauses in compound and complex sentences, and to explore them.

NLS coverage

Key objective

SL 6 To investigate clauses through:
- identifying the main clause in a long sentence
- investigating sentences which contain more than one clause
- understanding how clauses are connected (e.g. by combining three short sentences into one)

Learned through

TL Reading comprehension and writing composition
12, 13 To read and compare letters which inform
15 To consider layout and language
17 To draft, write, edit and present letters

Assessment criteria

SL By the end of this unit, pupils should be able to identify the main clause in a long sentence; combine clauses effectively in compound sentences.

TL Writing composition
Children should be able to write informative letters, adapting the language for the intended recipient.

Session 1

You will need OHT 18 and PCM 18A.

Shared reading

1 Talk to pupils about the types of official letter, e.g. from utilities companies, the local council. What sort of language would pupils expect? Give pupils two minutes to confer and note down predicted language features.

2 Display, read and talk about OHT 18. How would pupils react if they got this letter? What reactions do they think the writer anticipated? How can you tell from the wording of the letter?

3 Why does the writer begin the letter by mentioning modernization? Would this make a resident feel more positive about the cut-off?

Sentence level work

1 Reread the first paragraph and study the two sentences. What do pupils notice about punctuation in these sentences? (They are divided by commas.)

2 Remind pupils that sentences are made up of clauses, which are units of meaning within sentences. Each clause contains a verb or verb phrase. Some sentences have only one clause, but many have more than one. Main clauses can stand on their own; subordinate clauses cannot.

3 Investigate the first two sentences. One consists of two clauses, the other does not.
As part of our extensive modernization programme, we will be replacing old pipes in .... on Friday, June 12th.
In order to carry out this work, it will be necessary to cut off water supplies to domestic and commercial premises from 10a.m. – 3p.m. on that day.
Draw attention to the number of verbs in each sentence. The first sentence has only one verb phrase (*will be replacing*), the second sentence has two verb phrases (*to carry out / it will be necessary to cut off*).

4 Ask pupils which is the main clause in the second sentence. Remind them that the main clause can stand alone.

5 Consider other ways of combining these two clauses e.g.
It will be necessary to cut off water supplies to domestic and commercial premises from 10a.m. – 3p.m. on that day in order to carry out this work,
Discuss possible connectives, e.g. *so, because, when, and*. Which ones work well?

Independent activities

Pupils work on building sentences with main and subordinate clauses, using PCM 18A.

Plenary

Collect responses from pupils. Focus on the sequence of clauses in sentences, and check on punctuation. Have all pupils put the clauses in the same order? If not, consider which is most effective, asking pupils to explain their choices.

Session 2

You will need pupils' book 3, Unit 18, pages 42–3, and PCM 18B.

Shared reading

1 Discuss letters which are sent home from school. What is their purpose? Generate some examples of these types of letter.

2 Allow five minutes for the pupils to read the text from the pupils' book. Ask them to decide what they would think as a parent: would they think this trip a good idea? Allow two minutes for pupils to discuss this in pairs, then feedback to the rest of the class, challenging them to give reasons for their answers.

3 How do pupils think that children due to go on the trip would feel? Again, pupils should give reasons for their responses.

4 Discuss the overall impression the head teacher has tried to give in the letter. Would parents and children think that the trip is well organized, and will be successful? Encourage pupils to refer to the language used by the head teacher in giving their answers.

Sentence level work

1 Build on previous sessions by asking pupils to identify long and short sentences in the text. Look closely at these sentences, identifying:
   (a) which have more than one clause
   (b) whether the sentences are compound (two main clauses) or complex (one main clause and one or more subordinate clauses)
   (c) the main clause in complex sentences.
   For example:
   Children should bring a packed lunch and a drink, as this will save time at lunchtime. (complex sentence; connective – *as*)

Don't forget that they will be climbing on steep staircases, and walking on uneven surfaces! (compound sentence; connective – *and*)

2 Discuss which sentences are easier to understand, and experiment with rewriting the complex sentences as compound sentences, to see if this makes them easier or more difficult to read.

Independent activities

Children complete questions A and B in the pupils' book. Those who need additional practice may complete PCM 18B. Alternatively, this could be distributed for homework.

Plenary

Check the accuracy of identification of the main clauses, then ask pupils to report how easy they found it to identify complex sentences in other texts. Discuss whether some writers/types of text use more complex sentences than others. Why might this be?

Session 3

You will need pupils' book 3, Unit 18, pages 42–3, and the Reminder Sheet.

Shared writing

1 You are going to write an informative letter to a friend about a holiday outing you have arranged. Try to include as much information as possible.

2 Discuss what information should be included. Decide which is essential information. Consider what you can assume, e.g. will they need reminding to bring clean underwear or a toothbrush? Explain that the writer must work out what the reader will need to know, and include all this information.

3 Discuss the sequence for the information.

Write together

1 Model writing the first paragraph for activity C. Include complex sentences, discussing whether or not they are appropriate. Show how they are useful when giving reasons for an instruction.

2 Demonstrate how important it is to be accurate when using tenses. Which tense is appropriate for a letter about a forthcoming event? Probably the future tense, although there will be some use of the past tense (e.g. *as we agreed, …; I have booked…*)

3 Model correct use of punctuation, focusing on identifying boundaries between clauses.

Independent writing activity

Introduce the Reminder Sheet. Pupils can continue the letter themselves. Some may write their own opening paragraph. Encourage pupils to vary sentence length.

Plenary

Pupils work in pairs. Allow three or four minutes for pupils to read their partner's letter, and decide whether or not it is sufficiently informative, and whether the language is effective. As a class, build up a list of criteria for a successful informative letter.

Session 4

You will need pupils' book 3, Unit 18, pages 42–3, and the Reminder Sheet.

Shared writing

Explain that you are going to edit the information letters that were written in the previous session. Build up an editing checklist. Use the Reminder Sheet and the criteria discussed in the previous session as a prompt.

Write together

Model use of the editing checklist, going through the letter written in shared time, sentence by sentence. Make improvements as necessary, inviting pupils' contributions. Ensure they understand the function of punctuation in identifying boundaries between clauses.

Independent writing activity

Pupils apply the editing checklist to their own letters.

Plenary

Discuss the usefulness of a checklist. Is it an improvement on simply rereading a piece of work? How could pupils build up their own internal checklist? Remind pupils of their own personal targets as an aid to editing.

Assessment

Pupils should be able to:
• identify complex sentences in texts
• discriminate between compound and complex sentences
• identify the main clause in a complex sentence
• compose complex sentences, accurately punctuated
• plan, organize and write an informative letter.
They should use tenses accurately, and include complex sentences as appropriate.

Model answers

Pupils' book 3 ☐ A

1 That pupils are studying the Normans; the visit will improve their understanding.
2 So that parents will value the trip and agree to send their children.
3 Day out / time with friends / exciting / new place to visit.
4 So parents will ensure children wear appropriate footwear/clothing.
5 Answers will vary: nothing significant.
6 Answers will vary.

Pupils' book 3 ☐ B

7 *Children should bring a packed lunch and a drink*;
   Children… should take medication before leaving:
   … it will be one of the highlights of the school year.
8 Answers will vary.

☐ 18A   Investigating clauses 凵

Examples:
If you want to disconnect the supply to your old home, <u>you should give at least 14 days' notice.</u>
To get rid of gas, <u>open doors and windows.</u>
If the lid is not closed, or the bin is too heavy, <u>it cannot be emptied.</u>
If you have a complaint, <u>please contact us first.</u>
If you would like this leaflet in any other language or format, <u>please contact the City Council.</u>

☐ 18B   Recognizing the main clause 凵

Pupils should understand that the main clause of the sentence makes sense on its own; if they are struggling, prompt them to consider this.

Here are some main and subordinate clauses from information letters. See if you can match them to make complex sentences. Each complete sentence has one clause from column A, and one from column B.

■ Write out the sentences on the lines provided, or in your book.

■ Remember to punctuate the sentences using capital letters, full stops and commas.

■ Underline the main clause in each sentence.

■ When you have finished, see if there are any that can be improved, or changed around.

A	B
you should give at least 14 days' notice	it cannot be emptied
open doors and windows	please contact the City Council
if the lid is not closed, or the bin is too heavy	if you have a complaint
please contact us first	to get rid of gas
if you would like this leaflet in any other language or format	if you want to disconnect the supply to your old home

1 _____

_____

2 _____

_____

3 _____

_____

4 _____

_____

5 _____

_____

1 Read the sentences below. Underline the verb phrases, then highlight the main clause in each sentence. Remember that the main clause is the one that makes sense on its own.

> Realizing she was late, Angela rang her sister.
>
> John went on the ride again, despite feeling ill.
>
> As the rain fell more heavily, the level of water in the lake rose.
>
> James, who had overslept, was late for school.

Once you have completed these sentences, check with your partner.

2 Now go on to write some sentences containing main clauses. You could make them up yourself, or look for such sentences in the book you are reading at the moment.

Sentence	Written by:

18 *All about clauses*

- A sentence is made up of clauses.

- Some sentences have only one clause, for example:
   I have booked tickets for our holiday.

   We know there is only one clause here, because there is only one verb.

- Some sentences have more than one clause, for example:
   I have booked tickets for our holiday, and paid for them.

   We know that there is more than one clause here, because there are two verbs (*booked, paid*).

- In complex sentences, one of the clauses makes sense on its own, but the other(s) don't, for example:
   If you want to change the times, ring me at home.

   In this sentence, *ring me at home* is the main clause.

- The clauses can be written in a different order, for example:
   Ring me at home if you want to change the times.

   Ring me at home is still the main clause.

Links within sentences

The purpose of this unit is to encourage pupils to develop and extend their understanding of, and ability to use, conjunctions to write more complex sentences.

NLS coverage

Key objectives

SL 6 To understand how clauses are connected (e.g. by combining three short sentences into one)

SL 7 To use connectives to link clauses within sentences

Learned through

TL Reading comprehension and writing composition

14 To select and evaluate a range of texts, for persuasiveness, clarity and quality of information

19 To construct an argument in note form or full text to persuade others, and to present and evaluate the case

Assessment criteria

SL By the end of this unit, pupils should be able to combine short sentences into longer sentences using a variety of connectives; use the terms connectives and conjunctions appropriately.

TL Writing composition

Children should be able to write a persuasive letter.

Session 1

You will need OHT 19, PCM 19A and PCM 19B.

Shared reading

1 Ask pupils for examples of persuasive texts – adverts, letters etc. Which do they see most often? Explain that you will be looking at writing persuasively.

2 Display and read OHT 19 together. Ask pupils for their initial reactions. Do they agree with the writer? Are there any arguments the writer might have used but did not – e.g. loss of green space, environmental and wildlife issues.

3 Consider the other side of the argument. What about jobs that would be provided? Is the existing park not enough?

4 Ask pupils to reconsider their original decision.

5 Look at the ways in which the writer has tried to persuade the reader – creating a vision of an earthly paradise, his/her choice of words and images.

Sentence level work

1 Writers persuade people by choosing connectives carefully, to help readers follow their arguments.

2 The word 'connectives' describes anything that links clauses, sentences or paragraphs. Conjunctions are connectives; so are pronouns, some forms of punctuation and phrases. The focus in this unit is on conjunctions. Ask pupils to list conjunctions they use frequently. (*and, so, because,* etc.)

3 Select a sentence for investigation, for example:
Developers will move in and plough up The Field next week, unless the people of Marlesdene take action.

Identify the two clauses here, inviting a pupil to underline them in different colours. Can they now identify the conjunction? (It is *unless*.)

4 Experiment with altering the sequence of clauses, for example:
Unless the people of Marlesdene take action, developers will move in and plough up The Field next week.

Which sentence works better? *Unless* is still the conjunction, but it is not between the clauses.

5 Is there any other conjunction that would work here? Most other conjunctions require additional changes to the sentence, for example:
Developers will move in and plough up The Field next week, so the people of Marlesdene must take action.

6 Examine another sentence in the same way.

7 Generate sentences with structures similar to those you have investigated, for example:

The garden will quickly become overgrown, unless it is weeded every week.
The workers will be gone – replaced by robots.

8 Draw attention to the repetitive clause structure used to connect the clauses in this sentence:
Their children have played there, they have walked their dogs there, courted there, and played football and cricket there.

   This sentence is essentially a list of clauses with the same structure. The last clause is therefore linked by the conjunction *and*.

Independent activities

Pupils complete the same exercise, using PCM 19A and/or 19B. 19A asks pupils to identify connectives; 19B asks them to join shorter sentences into longer ones. It may be appropriate to offer 19B as homework.

Plenary

Discuss ways of connecting sentences, especially those they have identified or used. Which were most effective? Which do they think are most common? Explain that it is necessary to use a range of ways of connecting clauses to add variety.

Session 2

You will need pupils' book 3, Unit 19, pages 44–5, and PCM 19B (for those pupils who have not yet completed it).

Shared reading

1 Explain to pupils that you will be reading an extract from an appeal for a charity. What will the writer try to do? (To persuade people to donate money.) Discuss ways they might do this.

2 Allow pupils time to read the text to themselves, and to consider the approaches taken. Read the text to them. Identify strategies used to persuade the reader, e.g. describing the experience of blindness.

3 Discuss how pupils feel about the appeal, and why.

Sentence level work

1 One of the reasons this appeal is so effective is the way it draws the reader along. The writer has used connectives very cleverly to do this.

2 Ask pupils to pick out unusual sentence structures and investigate them, for example:

I still sometimes find myself groping anxiously for the bedside light when I'm staying in a strange hotel.
   Can this be split into two sentences?
I still sometimes find myself groping anxiously for the bedside light. I'm staying in a strange hotel.
   These sentences do not make sense in this order, or without changes. For example:
I sometimes stay in hotels. I find myself groping anxiously for the bedside light.

3 Draw attention to the changes which have to be made, e.g. the word *sometimes* has to be moved between clauses for them to have any link, and it is still unclear. Now rejoin these sentences:
When I stay in strange hotels I sometimes wake up in the night groping for the light.

4 How is this sentence connected to the previous ones in the original text? Look at the word *still*. Why does this link the sentences? Why is it more effective to place it at the beginning of the sentence? (It is nearer to the sentence with which it's linking.)

Independent activities

Children complete questions A and B in the pupils' book.

Plenary

Discuss the ways in which pupils have split and recombined sentences. Vote on the best versions.

Session 3

You will need pupils' book 3, Unit 19, pages 44–5, and the Reminder Sheet.

Shared writing

Explain that you will be writing a leaflet to support a local issue. Discuss the ways writers persuade people.

Write together

1 Plan the leaflet layout, then plot paragraphs.

2 Generate a list of connectives which pupils have encountered in persuasive texts. Remind pupils about the use of punctuation marks and pronouns to connect sentences within the text.

3 Demonstrate different ways of combining sentences into longer units, focusing on the effectiveness of each combination. Remind pupils about using different connectives, for example: *so, because, although, unless, however.*

Independent writing activity

1 Pupils write up their own leaflets.

2 Draw together and support pupils who have had difficulty with connecting sentences.

Plenary

Pupils display their work for others to comment on.

Session 4

You will need the draft from the previous shared writing session, or a pupil's draft, on OHT/flipchart.

Shared writing

1 Explain that you will be working to improve a piece of persuasive writing. Ask pupils to refer back to what they have already learned.

2 What types of connective do pupils expect to find between clauses? Draw out a list of connectives pupils have found in persuasive pieces they have written, and generate further examples. Emphasize language that implies: cause and effect, logical connectives, etc. Pupils should suggest: *so, because, therefore, it follows that, since, as; If … then…*

Write together

1 Remind pupils about the purpose of the text and to use the Reminder Sheet as a checklist. Ask them to identify particularly persuasive elements of the text.

2 Is there any point in the text at which it fails to convince? Investigate why. Are there better ways of linking clauses, e.g. by using stronger connectives, or by changing the punctuation. For example:
This is important to local people, because children need somewhere to play.
This is important to local people – children need somewhere to play!
  This strengthens the argument. (It changes the second clause from a reason into a statement of fact.)

3 Continue through the text finding places where similar strengthening could occur, making the piece more effective as a piece of persuasion.

Independent activity

Ask pupils to swap with a partner, and comment on each other's writing. They should then evaluate their own work and implement their partner's suggestions.

Plenary

Invite pupils to explain changes they made to their writing, and the impact this has had.

Assessment

Give feedback on the extent to which pupils:
• connect sentences effectively, using a range of conjunctions
• use persuasive devices
• structure the writing of persuasive pieces
• identify and improve weaker aspects of writing.

Model answers

Pupils' book 3 ☐ A

1 It helps to be able to see where you are, especially in a strange place.

2 Uses words like *panic stricken, terrified* and *nightmare* to emphasize his fear.

3 People might not know that they can have the operation, or be too scared to have it.

4 Donations to the campaign is the most likely.

5 Seeking medical advice is the main point.

Pupils' book 3 ☐ B

6 The first two should be broken down into two sentences, and the third into three. Check that they all make sense.

7 Answers will vary. Comment on use of connectives, and punctuation.

☐ 19A Collecting connectives ▯

should/<u>because</u>
tree/you, <u>By planting</u>
tree/you, <u>By planting</u>; insects/<u>and</u>
tree/you, <u>By planting</u>; better/<u>and</u>
better/<u>and</u> (note that the verb *will* applies to both clauses)

☐ 19B Using connectives ▯

Answers will vary. Most pupils will find conjunctions easy to use; more able pupils may also use punctuation and pronouns. Check that the combined sentences make sense.

1   Read through this text. Draw a line (/) between the clauses in each sentence, then underline the connectives.

Plant a Tree

Have you ever thought about planting a tree? You should, because there is no better way to help the planet.

By planting a tree, you will increase the amount of oxygen released into the air every day for people and animals to breathe.

By planting a tree, you will provide a habitat for birds and insects – and provide food for those creatures.

By planting a tree you will also make the area you live in look better, and feel better.

So... why not? Planting a tree is cheap and easy. It will make you feel better, and cheer up your neighbours too. What have you got to lose?

---

2   Remember that writers use a range of conjunctions in sentences. List them below:

_____

_____

_____

_____

_____

Using connectives

1 Read through this text. Combine some of the sentences, using the connectives you have found in other texts.

Healthy Eating!

How healthy is your diet? Lots of people don't have healthy diets. People eat too much fatty food, and too much sugar. What about you?

There are some foods people should eat every day. It is very important to eat fresh fruit and vegetables every single day. It is important to eat protein. It is important to eat carbohydrates.

People should eat foods that contain vitamins and minerals. Vitamins and minerals are found in many different foods.

_____

_____

_____

_____

_____

_____

_____

_____

2 Remember that you can connect sentences in different ways. When you have completed the first activity, fill in the following table:

Pronouns	
Words/phrases	
Punctuation	

19 *Choosing connectives*

One of the ways that writers persuade people is by choosing connectives really carefully. By doing this, they make it easier for readers to follow their arguments.

■ Connectives are words or phrases that link clauses, sentences or paragraphs. One of the ways that writers connect clauses and sentences is by choosing connective words and phrases. Connective words are called 'conjunctions'.

■ Writers can combine sentences in different ways to achieve different effects:

> *Developers will move in and plough up The Field next week, unless the people of Marlesdene take action.*

> *Unless the people of Marlesdene take action, developers will move in and plough up The Field next week.*

> *Developers will move in and plough up The Field next week, so the people of Marlesdene must take action.*

■ Writers must choose the best combination for each piece of writing.

■ Connectives you might wish to use are:

> *because   and   also   so   when   although   unless*
> *however   therefore   if   nevertheless   until   yet*

UNIT 20 *Trimming sentences*

The purpose of this unit is to encourage pupils to pick out the main ideas in sentences, and to identify what is not essential. They will then present the writing in a different way, taking into account the needs of their readers.

NLS coverage

Key objective

SL 2 To understand how writing can be adapted for different purposes, e.g. by changing sentence structures

Learned through

TL Reading comprehension
16 To fillet passages for relevant information and present ideas which are effectively grouped and linked

Assessment criteria

SL By the end of this unit, pupils should be able to identify different sentence types; identify the main idea in a sentence; trim sentences.

TL Writing composition
Children should be able to make notes on a text, and write these notes up into a form that is accessible to others who have not read the original.

Session 1

You will need OHT 20 and PCM 20A.

Shared reading

1 Explain that you are going to read an extract from a story. Ask them to think what sort of story it is.

2 Display and read OHT 20. Pupils may suggest a range of story types. Ask pupils who suggest traditional or folk tale to explain why. What clues are there?

3 Now look at the story itself. Identify the main characters. What are they like? Discuss the way Kipling writes. It is rather unusual, e.g. the opening sentence. Consider his individual use of words, e.g. *cavily*. What impact does this have? Discuss the imaginative and creative use of language.

Sentence level work

1 Discuss the audience for this story. Do pupils think it is aimed at people of any particular age? Look at the vocabulary Kipling has chosen, and the length of sentences. Look for complex and compound sentences. What do pupils find? Ask for specific examples – revise complex and compound sentences from previous units.

2 *He was not a Jute or an Angle, or even a Dravidian, which he might well have been.*

There are two clauses in this sentence. Can pupils identify the main clause? (the first one) Is the second clause necessary? If you were trying to simplify this story, you would not need the second part of the sentence at all, so that it would become: *He was not a Jute or an Angle, or even a Dravidian.*

3 Look at this sentence again. Is there any other way of simplifying it? Is it necessary at all? Would it be easier to say what he was rather than what he was not? Consider options.

4 Look at other sentences in the text: discuss which could be reduced, or simplified. Discuss possible changes, including splitting longer sentences into two, reducing unnecessary detail, etc.

Independent activities

Pupils should complete PCM 20A. This is a version of the OHT which pupils can adapt for younger pupils. When they have finished, ask one or two pupils to copy their versions onto a blank OHT for use in the plenary. Alternatively, photocopy onto OHT.

Plenary

Display and read the versions pupils have copied out. Discuss any differences between the two, particularly with respect to the intended audience. Identify changes pupils have made, focusing particularly on the changes to sentence length and structure.

Session 2

You will need pupils' book 3, Unit 20, pages 46–7, and PCM 20B.

Shared reading

1 Ask if pupils have seen a film version of *The Jungle Book*. Explain that this text is written by Rudyard Kipling, as was the OHT text. Do pupils think that the story in the book will be exactly the same as the story in the film(s)?

2 Ask pupils to turn to page 46 in the pupils' book and then read the text to them. Take initial responses. Is it what they expected? Discuss the differences in the story. What do pupils feel about the characters of Father Wolf and Shere Khan? What evidence is there for characterization?

Sentence level work

1 Remind pupils of what they worked on in the previous session. This time they will be looking at trimming sentences from this text. During the exercise, draw pupils' attention to separating plot and language. Take opportunities to remind pupils that this is more than just reducing the number of words – it is changing the story so that it is no longer Kipling's. Examine the way that reducing sentences impoverishes them.

2 Take the first sentence and look at it closely.

3 *The bushes rustled.* ~~a little in the thicket, and~~ *Father Wolf dropped* ~~with his haunches under him~~, *ready for his leap.*

   Here it has been broken down into two shorter ones, and some details taken out. What impact has this had on the sentence? (It has changed it from a compound sentence into two shorter sentences.)

4 Is there anything else that can be done to reduce it further? Does this contain the essential information?

Independent activities

Children complete questions A and B in the pupils' book. PCM 20B is preparation for the shared writing.

Plenary

Model comparing original and rewritten sentences, looking at sentence types. How many simple, compound and complex sentences can pupils find?

Session 3

You will need pupils' book 3, Unit 20, pages 46–7, a photocopy of page 46 for each pupil, and the Reminder Sheet.

Shared writing

Explain that what you have been practising is called 'précis'. What purposes could this have? Discuss the possibilities, e.g. in reviewing books, writing blurbs. In non-fiction, précis can help readers make accurate records of factual information which must be recalled. As a teacher, précis allows you to work out how much pupils have understood. Discuss why this is. Can pupils work it out? In order to cut the text down to essentials, readers must be able to identify the main ideas.

Write together

1 Distribute the photocopies and work through the first paragraph, identifying words that could be deleted. Keep on rereading the remaining text, to make sure it makes sense. Continue making reductions until pupils are clear that the essential ideas only are displayed.

2 Once you have completed the first paragraph, look at the sentence types which are left. What punctuation marks remain – is there any change here?

3 When there is a minimum amount of text remaining, check how it reads, comparing with the original. How might this be rewritten for younger children? What might be added to the text? Look at the difference between précis and simple story.

Independent writing activity

Pupils continue to rewrite this story, or another suitable text, for younger pupils, working through the two stages: précis then embellishment.

Plenary

Discuss with pupils what they have done to the précis texts to turn them into stories. Focus once more on sentence types. Has the balance of simple/compound/complex changed?

Session 4

You will need rewritten stories from the previous session, and the Reminder Sheet.

Shared writing

This is an opportunity to revise and improve the work already completed. Display and read together. Discuss the target audience, and how the text would meet their needs. Are there any points at which the text is unsuitable – either too simple or too challenging?

Write together

Adapt the text to improve the match between text and target reader. Focus particularly on sentence structure. Remind pupils that complex sentences with passive forms will be inappropriate for younger readers. You may also discuss vocabulary. Consider issues related to presentation of the text. How can this make a text more accessible for younger or less experienced readers? Discuss the use of different fonts / font sizes / spacing / illustration. Demonstrate using ICT.

Independent activity

Pupils continue working on their own version of the story, publishing using ICT where appropriate.

Plenary

Pupils discuss their layout decisions and the impact these had on the accessibility of the text.

Assessment

Comment on the extent to which pupils are able to:
• identify essential information in sentences
• identify simple/compound/complex stories
• précis accurately
• adapt précis to make a story.
Encourage pupils to comment on the types of changes they have made, and the impact the changes have had.

Model answers

Pupils' book 3 ☐ A

1 A child. She might have thought it was another animal.
2 He leapt because he was going to attack the thing (for food or to protect his family); when he saw it was a small child, he didn't want to hurt it.
3 She wants to keep him. We know because she talks *softly*, lets him suckle, and starts persuading her partner straight away.
4 Answers will vary: protect him from Shere Khan / raise him / eat him. Not all children will know the story. Their answers should be based on what they have read of the text so far.

Pupils' book 3 ☐ B

5 Answers will vary. Check that essential information is included. Encourage pupils to look again if they have not trimmed at least 50%.

☐ 20A   Adapting a story ▯

Children should take out some 'redundant' text that would entertain older readers but confuse younger ones; break longer sentences down into shorter sentences; adapt some vocabulary.

☐ 20B   Trimming sentences ▯

Children should reduce the text as far as possible and then write it out. As well as deletions, they may substitute words for phrases. There should be a greater proportion of simple and compound sentences in the reduced version.

Read the story again, and make changes to it that will make it easier for younger children to read.

How the first letter was written

Once upon a most early time was a Neolithic man. He was not a Jute or an Angle, or even a Dravidian, which he might well have been. He was a primitive, and he lived cavily in a cave, and he wore very few clothes, and he couldn't read and he couldn't write and he didn't want to, and except when he was hungry he was quite happy. His name was Tegumai and his wife's name was Teshumai, and his little girl-daughter's name was Taffy. And she was Tegumai's Best Beloved and her own Mummy's Best Beloved, and she was not spanked half as much as was good for her; and they were all three very happy. As soon as Taffy could run about she went everywhere with her Daddy Tegumai, and sometimes they would not come home to the Cave till they were hungry, and then Teshumai would say, 'Where in the world have you two been, to get so shocking dirty? Really, my Tegumai, you're no better than my Taffy.'

From *Just So Stories* by Rudyard Kipling (Macmillan, London, 1950), reprinted by permission of A.P. Watt Ltd on behalf of The National Trust for Places of Historical Interest or Natural Beauty.

20B *Trimming sentences*

1 Look at this extract from *The Jungle Book*. Delete unnecessary words. Use what is left to write out a short story.

The bushes rustled a little in the thicket, and Father Wolf dropped with his haunches under him, ready for his leap. Then, if you had been watching, you would have seen the most wonderful thing in the world – the wolf checked in mid-spring. He made his bound before he saw what it was he was jumping at, and then he tried to stop himself. The result was that he shot up straight into the air for four or five feet, landing almost where he left ground.

"Man!" he snapped. "A man's cub. Look!"

From *The Jungle Book* by Rudyard Kipling (Macmillan Centenary Edition, 1982), reprinted by permission of A.P. Watt Ltd on behalf of The National Trust for Places of Historical Interest or Natural Beauty.

2 Write out the story in as few words as you can:

_____

_____

_____

_____

3 Look at the sentences you have written. Compare the number of each with the original.

	Original	Simplified
Simple sentences		
Compound sentences		
Complex sentences		

Trimming sentences

There are many reasons for trimming sentences.

- Sometimes, we need to remember essential information. Trimming details helps us to do this.

- Sometimes we don't have the time or the space to write down everything, so we have to trim details.

Whenever we trim sentences, it is important that readers will be able to work out what the text means. Sometimes we have to change words to help us do this.

For example:

> The bushes rustled a little in the thicket, and Father Wolf dropped with his haunches under him, ready for his leap.

> The bushes rustled. Father Wolf dropped, ready for his leap.

> The bushes rustled. Father Wolf got ready to leap.

UNIT 21 *Links between sentences*

The purpose of this unit is for pupils to develop and extend their understanding of, and ability to manipulate, conjunctions to write more complex sentences.

NLS coverage

Key objective

SL 7 To use connectives to link sentences in longer texts

Learned through

TL Reading comprehension
15 To collect and investigate use of persuasive devices

TL Writing composition
18 To write a commentary on an issue, setting out and justifying a personal view; to set out and link points, e.g. numbered lists, bullet points

Assessment criteria

SL By the end of this unit, pupils should be able to identify linking devices between sentences; use the term 'connective' appropriately; link sentences in their own writing.

TL Writing composition
Children should be able to design a poster / web page to support an argument.

Session 1

You will need OHT 21, PCM 21A and PCM 21B.

Shared reading

1 During this unit, pupils will be looking at two persuasive texts – an article and a website. Review the range of persuasive texts they have already encountered, including TV adverts and jingles.

2 Explain that you will be looking at how persuasion can change a reader's point of view, and thereby their behaviour. There are many examples of texts that aim to do this. Ask pupils if they can think of any media texts that aim to change, for example, driving behaviour.

3 Display and read OHT 21. Ask pupils for their initial reactions. Do they agree with the writer?

4 List the arguments the writer cites against having a long summer holiday. Do children agree with them? Are there any others s/he could have used? Which arguments are most convincing? (Think of potential reader groups.) Return to the text for evidence. Ask pupils to reconsider their original response – have they changed their minds?

5 Look at how the writer has tried to persuade readers – focusing on boredom for pupils and expense for parents. Who do pupils think is the intended audience for this piece?

Sentence level work

1 Writers use connectives to build up powerful arguments. Connectives link clauses, sentences or paragraphs. This unit focuses on linking sentences and paragraphs.

2 Begin with the first paragraph. Children reread it and then, in pairs, discuss words and phrases which refer to the passage of time. Allow three minutes for this. Invite one pair to identify what they have found. Discuss whether any more parts of the paragraph could be highlighted, e.g.
The long summer break is nearly upon us once more! Within a very short time, school children will be released from school for six whole weeks.

3 Discuss how the writer has emphasized the length of the holiday – e.g. by using the words *whole* and *released*. Why might the writer have used these words? What does this tell us about the audience?

4 Allow pupils to scan the third paragraph for linking devices. Invite them to underline links on the OHT. Notice how the writer has used the sequences *first day – second day – third day* to link the sentences. Why has the writer selected *third week*? This links back to the sequence of numbers.

5 Look for other linking devices (e.g. repetition of the word *families* in the fourth paragraph, use of *more*, and in the final paragraph a return to the theme of time with *after six weeks*).

Independent activities

Pupils complete a similar exercise, using PCM 21A and/or 21B. 21A asks pupils to identify links between sentences; 21B asks them to link sentences and paragraphs. Pupils may complete one or both. It may be appropriate to offer 21B as homework.

Plenary

Discuss the ways of linking sentences that pupils have identified in PCM 21A or used in PCM 21B. Which were most effective at building up the arguments? Which are easiest to use? Remind pupils that using links in this way helps to emphasize arguments.

Session 2

You will need pupils' book 3, Unit 21, pages 48–9, and PCM 21B, for those pupils who have not yet completed it.

Shared reading

1 Explain to pupils that you will be reading a page from a website. What features might they expect to find in a web page but not in a magazine article?

2 Ask pupils to turn to page 48 in the pupils' book. Allow them time to skim this copy of a web page. Ask them to jot down any unfamiliar terms. Before reading it aloud, instruct pupils to follow the text carefully and listen for those terms, because hearing the item read aloud might help them to work out the meaning. After reading, tackle any difficult vocabulary before moving on.

3 Discuss pupils' responses to the web page. How do they feel about it, and why?

4 The writer has linked vegetarianism to healthy eating. How convincing is the argument? Is there any supporting evidence? Note the way the writer refers to *research* and uses technical terms to emphasize the scientific basis of the work.

5 Discuss the impact of the web page, its intended audience, and the use of colour and illustration.

Sentence level work

1 Focus on the first panel of the web page. Draw attention to the use of bullet points to link ideas. Discuss why this is effective. (In this argument, all of the points share the same opening which is effectively repeated. This gives it much greater emphasis.) In addition, the bullet points are separated from the rest of the text – they stand out because of the layout.

2 Now look at the second section of text. Discuss ways in which the sentences are linked, often by contrast. Consider the contrast between *well-balanced* and *chips and chocolate*. This is emphasized by the use of the word *either*. Draw attention to the way in which the words *health* and *healthy* are repeated.

Independent activities

Children complete questions A and B in the pupils' book.

Plenary

Ask pupils to contribute linked sentences they have found in their current reading texts. They should explain how the sentences are linked, and why they think the writer has chosen that particular link.

Session 3

You will need pupils' book 3, Unit 21, pages 48–9, and the Reminder Sheet.

Shared writing

1 Explain that you will be writing a poster or web page to persuade people to change their behaviour. In the class example, you will be trying to persuade readers to use cars less and cycle instead. In individual pieces of writing, pupils may select their own issue. This would be a good opportunity to link in with other areas of the curriculum, e.g. environmental, health or relationship issues.

2 Begin by identifying where this text will appear and its audience. Is the idea to persuade adults, or to suggest that children raise these issues with their parents? Remind pupils how important it is to decide on the audience, purpose and context before writing begins.

3 Next, start planning out points in favour of driving less / cycling more. Remind pupils that it is only necessary to include ideas, which will appeal to the intended audience.

Write together

1 Plan the layout of the poster / web page, then plot out paragraphs.

2 Review the different types of link encountered in shared reading and preceding lessons.

3 Demonstrate the writing of the first paragraph. Focus on the use of connectives to build up the main argument.

Independent writing activity

Pupils work on their own posters / web pages. Support pupils who need help with linking sentences.

Plenary

Place a few sheets of self-stick note-paper on each desk and ask pupils to leave out their drafts for others to read. Constructive comments should be written on the note-paper and stuck to the draft. Allow two minutes at the end of the session for pupils to read the comments.

Session 4

You will need the draft from the previous Shared writing session.

Shared writing

Work on completion of the draft for the poster. Review the arguments and reread the opening paragraph.

Write together

1 Continue writing, taking and commenting on contributions from pupils. Focus on the extent to which they have used strong links between their suggestion and the rest of the text.

2 When you have finished, reread the whole text, strengthening links where possible.

Independent activity

Pupils complete their own writing, using ideas and suggestions from previous sessions. Once the text is complete, they should consider publishing options – laying out the page or beginning a web page design.

Plenary

Invite pupils to explain the links they have made and how they feel this has supported their arguments.

Assessment

Give feedback on the extent to which pupils:
• identify linking devices used by writers
• link sentences effectively
• use persuasive devices
• structure the writing of persuasive pieces
• identify and improve weaker aspects of writing.

Model answers

Pupils' book 3 ◻ **A**

1 Answers will vary, but pupils should justify their choices.
2 No – chips and chocolate are not healthy.
3 Mostly salad and raw vegetables.
4 The phrase is intended as an insult. It implies the food is not fit for people. It is used to annoy vegetarians, so they have used it here to respond.
5 Food based on cereals.
6 Fats, oils and sweets.

Pupils' book 3 ◻ **B**

7 Answers will vary. Check on the layout, and the use of bullet points.
8 Answers will vary.

◻ **21A   Finding the links** ▯

Pupils should identify the following connectives: temporal (*now; on Sunday; After the first day; At the end of; By the; After*); logical (*By; so*); contrasting (*But*); linking (*and*). They may identify some other linking devices, e.g. *Here's how.*

◻ **21B   Linking ideas** ▯

Pupils should use 21A as a model; this will support those who are struggling. Encourage a range of connectives.

Read through this text. Underline or highlight links between sentences. When you have finished, list the different types of connective you found.

Run for Charity

Summer holidays are just on the horizon: now is the time to get in shape for those lazy days on the beach.

You can get in great shape – and raise money for charity. Here's how.

On Sunday July 29th there will be a 5km Fun Run for parents of children at St Anthony's. By getting sponsorship, you can raise money for new windows in the school.

But how will that get you in shape? Mrs Smith will be starting a running club for those who want to get fit for the run. Who knows, it could be the start of a whole new you!

After the first day, you might be stiff. At the end of the second run, you'll never want to go again. But by the third or fourth run you will start to enjoy it, and after your third or fourth Fun Run – there'll be no stopping you!

So come on – wear that bikini (or Bermuda shorts) with pride. Run for your summer!

21ʙ Linking ideas

This is the plan for a poster advertising a swimming club. Paragraph headings have been written. Your job is to write the paragraphs. Remember to link sentences so that the arguments are more powerful.

Swimming Club

There is a new swimming club

You could get yourself fit

You could make new friends

There are many benefits

List the links you have used:

Links between sentences

1 One of the ways that writers persuade people is by using connectives to link ideas to build powerful arguments. Examples of links are: conjunctions, pronouns, some forms of punctuation and repetition. For example:

> *The <u>long</u> summer break is <u>nearly upon us once more</u>! <u>Within a very short time</u>, school children will be released from school for <u>six whole weeks</u>.*

Here, the writer has emphasized the length of the holiday.

2 Sometimes, writers build up a sequence using numbers. For example:

> *Everyone enjoys their <u>first day</u> relaxing, eating and reading, watching cartoons on TV. Most enjoy the <u>second day</u>. But by <u>day three</u> the novelty is beginning to wear off. By <u>week three</u>…*

3 Another linking device is the repetition of words. For example:
> *… school children will be released from school for <u>six whole weeks</u>.*

> <u>*Six weeks*</u> *is a very long time.*

> <u>*After six weeks*</u> *of lazing about…*

4 Writers can also use a list of bullet points to link related ideas. Each related idea starts with a bullet point, and begins in the same way. The sentences are linked because they all begin in the same way. For example:

> *By cycling to school you could:*
> - *save money on the bus fare*
> - *improve your fitness*
> - *build up the muscles in your legs.*

5 Sentences can be linked by contrast. Consider the contrast between *well-balanced* and *chips and chocolate*.

Prepositions

The purpose of this unit is to introduce pupils to, and explore, the idea of prepositions and prepositional phrases which describe the relationship between objects and ideas.

NLS coverage

Key objective

SL 3 To search for, identify and classify a range of prepositions; experiment with substituting different prepositions and their effect on meaning. Understand and use the term preposition

Learned through

TL **Reading comprehension and writing composition**
4, 5 To read, rehearse and modify the performance of poetry; to select poetry and justify their choices
11 To use performance poems as models to write, and to produce polished poetry by revising, redrafting and presenting

Assessment criteria

SL By the end of this unit, pupils should be able to identify a range of prepositions and prepositional phrases; classify and sort prepositions and prepositional phrases; use prepositions effectively in their writing, selecting from a range.

TL **Writing composition**
Children should be able to write performance poems based on those they have read, in a polished form for publication and presentation.

Session 1

You will need OHT 22, PCM 22A and PCM 22B.

Shared reading

1 Explain to pupils that you will be reading a poem about friendship. Do any of them have best friends? Have they always had the same best friend? Have they ever fallen out with a friend? How did it feel? Tell pupils that you will be asking them to decide how old the 'voice' of the poem is.

2 Display OHT 22. Read the poem 'Best friends' aloud to the children. Invite them to read along with you. Encourage them to use expression in reading.

3 Discuss the initial question about the age of the 'voice'. Ask pupils for their responses, and for explanations for their answers. Discuss together, and come to an agreement.

4 Ask pupils to:
- name two things they like in a best friend
- decide which is the best reason the writer gives.

Sentence level work

1 Ask pupils to name the writer's current best friend. How do they know? Who was the previous best friend? Look at how they know this (s/he talks to / sits next to). Draw attention to the word *to*. Explain that this is a preposition, and that prepositions explain relationships between things.

2 Reread the poem; ask pupils to identify prepositions as you do so. Underline the prepositions. Look at the different types of preposition in the poem. Many of them define physical relationships between the children in the poem.

3 Begin a chart to show the different types of preposition, such as:

time	*before*
position	*next to*
direction	*to*
means	*by*
possession	*of*
accompaniment	*with*

Independent activities

1 Direct pupils to PCM 22A. Read through the poem 'Good Company'.

2 The pupils' task is to underline the prepositions in the poem. Offer an alternative to pupils who may find this text too challenging, or insufficiently challenging. Those who complete the underlining may go on to PCM 22B which asks them to classify the poem's prepositions.

Plenary

Add the prepositions found in the poem to the original list. Discuss which are the most common.

Session 2

You will need pupils' book 3, Unit 22, pages 50–51.

Shared reading

Turn to the poem 'Billy McBone' in the pupils' book. Read it through two or three times, perhaps using pupil volunteers on the second and third readings. Then take pupils' initial reactions. For example:

- How do the pupils feel about Billy?
- How would they describe Billy's character?
- Can they identify unusual words in the poem?
- What do they think of the poet's choice of words, e.g. *burgle*?

Sentence level work

1 Reread the poem and quickly identify prepositions.

2 Explain that sentences containing prepositions can be analysed into:

subject	verb	prepositional phrase, for example:
I	*walked*	*to school.*
She	*ran*	*away from the monster.*
I	*dressed*	*before breakfast.*
They	*went home*	*on the bus.*
Sandra	*ate*	*with Tony.*

3 Ask pupils to generate sentences which have this structure. Experiment with different types of preposition.

Independent activities

Children complete questions A and B in the pupils' book, which enable them to practise the skills of identifying and generating prepositional phrases.

Plenary

During the plenary, practise substituting prepositions and investigate the effect of this. For example:

I	*walked*	*from school.*
She	*ran*	*towards the monster.*
I	*dressed*	*after breakfast.*
They	*went home*	*by bus.*
Sandra	*ate*	*after Tony.*

Session 3

You will need pupils' book 3, Unit 22, pages 50–51, and the Reminder Sheet.

Shared writing

1 Explain that you are going to write a poem based on experiences in school, using 'Best friends' as a model. Ask pupils whether they think the 'voice' of this poem is male or female. You are going to transform it to a poem about male friendship.

2 Begin by generating a list of possible names and activities. Remind pupils about the prepositions they may use (e.g. play *with*; send e-mails *to*; call *for*).

3 Try to use a range of prepositions – refer to the chart generated in Session 1 for ideas.

Write together

Begin to compose a poem, using male names and the activities generated. This is a short poem, and it should be possible to complete it in one shared session.

Independent writing activity

Following on from the shared writing, pupils can either polish the version that you have written together or use the suggestion in activity C of the pupils' book. Encourage them to exchange work to gain other pupils' perspectives on the poem.

Plenary

Listen to several poems. Ask pupils to comment on the content and vocabulary, as well as rhythm and rhyme. Invite comments on the range of prepositions; select some examples and expand prepositional phrases.

Assessment

Pupils should be able to:
- use the terms 'preposition' and 'prepositional phrase' accurately in discussion
- identify prepositions and prepositional phrases
- categorize prepositions
- use prepositions in their own writing
- write a poem using a known poem as a model.

Model answers

Pupils' book 3 ☐ A

1 Teachers probably thought he was stupid. This is what Ahlberg implies. Pupils may also infer that teachers thought him lazy.

2 No, because he probably behaved differently outside class.

3 It is as if his body is in prison, but his mind is not. The phrase reminds us of an animal. His mind is not in the classroom.

4 Answers will vary. It might be someone who didn't like school.

5 Answers will vary.

Pupils' book 3 ☐ B

6 Make sure that pupils have correctly identified parts of the sentence.

7 Pupils could use sentences from the poem as models.

☐ 22A   Prepositions ⒫

<u>at</u> the top of the house; <u>with</u> a flea; <u>by</u> a thread… <u>from</u> the ceiling; <u>at</u> work… <u>on</u> the; <u>of</u> his web…; up <u>in</u>; <u>as</u> he weaves… <u>as</u> he dangles; <u>up</u> to; <u>down</u> to… <u>below</u>; <u>when</u>; <u>in</u> my room

☐ 22B   Prepositions ⒫

time: *as, when*
position: *at, by, on, in, up, down, below*
direction: *towards*
means: *by*
possession: *of*
accompaniment: *with*

Poetic prepositions

Read this poem.
Underline or highlight the prepositions in the poem.

GOOD COMPANY

I sleep in a room at the top of the house

With a flea, and a fly, and a soft-scratching mouse,

And a spider that hangs by a thread from the ceiling,

Who gives me each day such a curious feeling

When I watch him at work on the beautiful weave

Of his web that's so fine I can hardly believe

It won't all end up in such terrible tangles,

For he sways as he weaves, and spins as he dangles.

I cannot get up to that spider, I know,

And I hope he won't get down to me here below,

And yet when I wake in the chill morning air

I'd miss him if he were not still swinging there,

For I have in my room such good company,

There's him, and the mouse, and the fly, and the flea.

LEONARD CLARK

'Good Company' by Leonard Clark,
reprinted by permission of Robert Clark, Literary Executor.

22B Prepositions

Types of preposition

Use the table below to sort the prepositions from the poem into categories.

Once you have finished, try to think of some other prepositions.
Write these in a different colour.

Preposition type	
time	
position	
direction	
means	
possession	
accompaniment	

22 Prepositions

1 A preposition is a word which describes the relationship between two objects, events or ideas.

2 There are different types of preposition.

Preposition type	Example
time	after, before, at, during
position	in, on, by
direction	to, from, over
means	by
possession	of
accompaniment	with

3 Prepositions are found in prepositional phrases, for example:
I walked <u>from school</u>.
She ran <u>towards the monster</u>.
I dressed <u>after breakfast</u>.
They went home <u>by bus</u>.
Sandra ate <u>after Tony</u>.

UNIT 23 *Varying sentence openings*

The purpose of this unit is for pupils to investigate ways of opening sentences. This will allow them to extend the range of sentence structures they use, considering the needs of the reader.

NLS coverage

Key objectives

SL 2 To understand how writing can be adapted for different audiences, e.g. by changing vocabulary and sentence structures
SL 7 To use connectives between and within sentences, and as sentence openers

Learned through

TL Reading comprehension and writing composition
6 To explore the challenge and appeal of older literature
9 To write in the style of the author

Assessment criteria

SL By the end of this unit, pupils should be able to vary sentence openings and structures for different purposes.

TL Writing composition
Pupils should be able to write in the style of an author, using typical structures and language.

Session 1

You will need OHT 23 and PCM 23A.

Shared reading

1 The text is an adapted extract from C.S. Lewis's *The Voyage of the Dawn Treader*. Have any pupils read other books by Lewis? Discuss the books, and the fantasy and adventure elements they contain.

2 Display and read OHT 23. Allow pupils to read the text again on their own. How do they think Lucy would be feeling? How would they feel?

Sentence level work

1 Now look at the language used in this text, which has been pared down from the original version, with much of the detail taken out. Has the writer really conveyed Lucy's feelings? What it might be like to be in the middle of such a storm? How might the writing be changed to make it more descriptive?

2 Draw pupils' attention to sentence construction. Look at the first word in each sentence. Pupils should notice that many of the sentences begin with *The*. Discuss what impact this has on the text. Look at other sentences, and highlight the subject.

In how many sentences is the subject at the beginning? Now, using a different colour, highlight the verb. Discuss the pattern of each sentence. Most of them are subject – verb – object.

3 Reread the text, then discuss ways of varying sentences. Some pupils will suggest adding detail, e.g. adjectives/adverbs, and varying/strengthening verbs. Also discuss ways of altering the basic structure of the sentences, e.g. by introducing with an adverbial phrase, such as *Later that morning*.

4 Generate a list of possible sentence openers, including adverbial phrases. Remind pupils that adverbial phrases answer *when? where? how? how often?*

Independent activities

Distribute PCM 23A which offers one sentence with a range of different openings. Pupils decide which is the most effective, and why. PCM 23B is an alternative activity that allows pupils to trawl current readers for sentence starters that they find interesting.

Plenary

Explain that there is no *correct* choice in PCM 23A. Discuss pupils' choices of sentence. How many made the same choice? Group pupils by first choice, and ask them to agree one reason for their decision.

Session 2

You will need pupils' book 3, Unit 23, pages 52–3, and OHT 23.

Shared reading

1 Explain that you will be reading Lewis's original version of the episode encountered in the previous session. What differences do pupils expect?

2 Ask pupils to turn to page 52 in the pupils' book. Read the text aloud so that they can follow it. Allow pupils some time to reread the text on their own.

3 Discuss how the storm is described. Consider the senses to which Lewis appeals. Ask pupils to look for evidence of:
Vision (*Lucy… saw a great rack of clouds; yellow sunset poured through; waves… took unusual shapes* etc.)
Hearing (*… the very noise of the wind…*)
Taste and smell (none)
Touch/Movement (*The ship seemed to move uneasily; The air grew cold; … deeper down than she would have believed possible* etc.)

4 Discuss the main senses appealed to here – sight and movement. Why is this?

5 Revisit the OHT text. How do pupils feel about it now?

Sentence level work

1 Explain to pupils that you will be looking at the way Lewis begins sentences. Remind them that, in the OHT version, most sentences began with the subject. Are there any sentences like that in this version? There is one: *The air grew cold.* What about the others?

2 Note what Lewis has done with sentences which begin with the subject. (He has expanded them.) Very few now begin *The.* Draw attention to other details, e.g. his use of alliteration (*A great grey hill of water…*)

3 Look at sentences which do not begin with the subject. Many begin with adverbs (*Then / While / Before*) or adverbial phrases (*Up aloft… / There came an evening when…*). Make sure pupils understand that connectives are often adverbials, because they are linked most strongly to the verb in the sentence.

4 Compare sentences with their 'stripped' version in the OHT text. What impact does varying the opening have on each sentence, and on the text as a whole?

5 Return to the sentence *The air grew cold.* Why has Lewis chosen to leave this sentence as a very simple structure? What impact does it have amongst the more complex sentences? Do pupils feel that it adds an impression of suddenness, or contrast?

6 Ask pupils to discuss some elements of Lewis's style.

Independent activities

Children complete A and B in the pupils' book.

Plenary

Look at sentence rewrites. Do pupils have one they feel is an improvement on the original? Why/why not?

Session 3

You will need pupils' book 3, Unit 23, pages 52–3, and the Reminder Sheet.

Shared writing

You will be writing about an adventure, using elements of Lewis's style. The episode you will be writing will be about characters involved in a disaster. Give a background summary. This may be one you have created yourself. Otherwise, use the following outline:
A child (Tariq) is on his way to his grandmother's house with his parents. The car has broken down, and they are walking to the nearest garage. They realize a thunder storm is building up. They can see nowhere to shelter, and they have come a long way from the car.

Write together

1 Remind pupils of the senses to which Lewis appealed in his writing: mainly touch/movement and sight, with some hearing. Ask pupils for some phrases which may describe the storm building up. Expand these sentences, e.g.
They could hear thunder.
They could hear cracks of thunder.
In the distance, they could hear cracks of thunder. The cracks were coming closer!

2 Build up a range of these, varying the sentence openings. Refer back to the list of possibilities from Session 1, and use the pupils' book text for ideas.

3 Begin to put these together. Discuss ways of sequencing the ideas (they should be chronologically sequenced because this is a narrative). Many of the sentence openings will therefore answer the question *when?*

4 Explain to pupils that you are aiming for a text of similar length to the extract from *The Voyage of the Dawn Treader* – short but perfectly formed!

Independent writing activity

Allow pupils to work on their own ideas. They can use the model scenario or invent their own. Remind them to refer to two or more senses.

Plenary

Ask pupils to select sentences of which they are proud. Ask other pupils to comment, and explain why they like the sentence, or how it may be improved.

Session 4

You will need one sample piece, written by a pupil, on OHT, and the Reminder Sheet.

Shared writing

Read the sample piece to the class. Explain that you will be revising and editing the piece together.

Write together

1 Focus on variety of sentence structure, and openings. Remind pupils how, in the original, Lewis left some sentences very short and simple – for contrast.

2 Consider the piece with pupils, referring to the original text and working on variations of sentences.

3 Once the piece is revised, remind pupils to check for grammatical agreement, spelling, punctuation, etc.

Independent writing activity

Pupils complete and revise their own work.

Plenary

1 Pupils exchange pieces of writing with their partners, and read. Ask them to select their favourite part from their partner's work, and share it with them.

2 Discuss how easy they found it to vary sentence openings. Did their final pieces bear any similarities to Lewis's writing?

Assessment

Comment on the extent to which pupils:
• are able to identify sentence elements – subject, verb, object, adverb / adverbial phrase
• use a variety of ways to begin and structure sentences
• work to improve their own writing
• are able to imitate the style of an author.

Model answers

Pupils' book 3 ▭ A

1 Answers will vary: pupils may refer to the timescale. Lewis writes as if all these things happen one after the other. He also uses words like *torn*.

2 She was fascinated, and stood watching it. Pupils should note that she did not move until she was told to – it seems as though she didn't think of it.

3 Answers will vary.

4 Lucy didn't know what had to be done. Most pupils should realize that she might be physically in the way, because things had to be done quickly, and she couldn't predict what or when. Some may see that she might distract the sailors because they would be worried about her.

5 The ship was moving, and lots of things were happening. She would need to find things to hold onto.

Pupils' book 3 ▭ B

6 Answers will vary. Encourage pupils to do more than simply change a couple of words. They should try to make sentences as different as possible, whilst retaining the sense, and be able to justify their choice.

▭23A Varying sentence openings ▯
Focus on pupils' explanation for their choice of opener.

▭23B Varying sentence openings ▯
Focus on pupils' explanation for their choice of opener.

Sentence openings

This opening sentence from an adventure story is written in several different ways. Choose the one you think is the most effective, then place the others in order.

When you have finished, write about the most effective sentence, explaining why you have chosen this particular one.

A dog barked

The dog barked.	
In the middle of the night, the dog barked.	
Startled by the sudden noise, the dog barked.	
For the third day in succession, the dog barked.	
Somewhere in the distance, a dog barked.	
The silence was broken when the dog barked.	
On the television, a dog barked.	
The baby cried, the hoover hummed, the dog barked.	
The dog – a large Labrador – barked.	

Explain the reasons for your first choice.

_____

_____

_____

_____

_____

_____

Collecting sentence openings

Use this grid to collect examples of different sentence openers from adventure stories. Make a note of where you found each sentence. Write a brief explanation of why you selected each one.

Sentence	Source	Comment

23 *Varying sentence openings*

Writers use a variety of different sentence types and sentence openings because this keeps the reader interested.

Many sentences begin with adverbs or adverbial phrases. These answer the questions: *when? where? how often? how?*

when?	There came an evening when Lucy… While she was noting these things… Before they had finished…
where?	Up aloft… In the distance… Nearby…
how often?	Every Sunday … Occasionally …
how?	By holding on tightly, they managed…

In a **narrative**, most of the sentence openings will relate to **when** things happen.

UNIT 24 *Punctuating complex sentences*

The purpose of this unit is for pupils to further develop their understanding of complex sentences, and to increase the accuracy of their punctuation.

NLS coverage

Key objective
[SL] 4 To use punctuation marks accurately in complex sentences

Learned through
[TL] **Reading comprehension and writing composition**
6 To explore the challenge and appeal of older literature: listening to texts being read aloud; reading extracts from classic serials shown on television; discussing differences in language used
9 To write in the style of an author

Assessment criteria
[SL] By the end of this unit, pupils should be able to identify and compose complex sentences; identify punctuation marks used; punctuate complex sentences accurately.

[TL] **Reading comprehension and writing composition**
Children should be able to identify features of a writer's style, and incorporate some of these into their own writing.

Session 1
You will need OHT 24 and PCM 24A.

Shared reading
1 Explain that you will be working with texts written by Lewis Carroll, whose first book for children, *Alice's Adventures in Wonderland*, was written in 1865. Can they think of any other authors who were writing this long ago? What do they expect? Briefly discuss the role of books and storytelling in a time when there was no radio/TV/PCs, etc.

2 Ask pupils if they know anything about *Alice's Adventures in Wonderland*. Some may have read it, had it read to them or seen a film version.

3 Display and read OHT 24. Did Alice make the right decision? Why? Would they have done the same? What do the flavours in the drink tell us about the time when Carroll was writing? (They were the best things to eat.) What would be the flavours now?

4 What might Alice have expected to happen? What do pupils think will happen?

Sentence level work
1 Explain you are going to investigate this text. Count how many sentences are in this extract – only three.

The second sentence has 109 words in it! Do pupils write sentences like this? Was it easy to understand? Now discuss how Carroll has made this sentence comprehensible. Begin by looking at how many different sorts of punctuation he has used in this sentence. (There are: commas, quotation marks, inverted commas, brackets, semi-colons and colons – as well as a capital letter and a full stop.) Carroll also used italics for emphasis.

2 Break the sentence down into units, marking breaks on the OHT with a slash.
   Draw children's attention to verbs and punctuation if they have difficulties.

3 Focus in particular on more unusual punctuation marks, for example, the colon. Pupils may have used colons before to introduce lists. The colon in this sentence is introducing a list of rules children should have learned. Children should also notice that the items in Alice's list are separated by semi-colons.

Independent activities
Explain that children will be experimenting to see how long they can make one sentence without losing the sense of it. Distribute PCM 24A. Pupils who finish can look for the longest sentence they can find in other texts. Each group should write their best sentence onto an OHT for the plenary.

Plenary

1 Display and discuss sentences. Focus on how well the writers have used punctuation to sustain meaning and links between elements of the sentence. Which is the longest sentence, and does it work?

2 If any pupils found long sentences in other stories, ask them to read them out, using the punctuation to help them. Did the punctuation help?

Session 2

You will need pupils' book 3, Unit 24, pages 54–5, and PCM 24B.

Shared reading

1 You will be reading another extract from *Alice's Adventures in Wonderland*. What have pupils learned of Carroll's style?

2 What do they think might happen in this extract, which comes from a section later in the book? They will remember that the previous extract involved magic potions; could Carroll use the same device again?

3 Read the text to the pupils, and discuss it. Would they have drunk another potion? Can they work out the result of drinking the previous potion from this extract? How might it feel to be growing larger and larger?

Sentence level work

1 Look for the shortest and longest sentence. The shortest is easy – only one word! How about the longest? The first sentence contains 70 words.

2 Look at this sentence in some detail. The colon links two main parts of the sentence. Carroll could have used a full stop followed by a capital letter. Try rereading the sentence in this way. Do pupils prefer it as one or two sentences, and why? Why do they think Carroll chose to make the sentence so long?

3 Look at other places in which Carroll has used a colon: are they the same?

4 Focus on other punctuation marks, and discuss why Carroll has used them. What is their function? Show how they mark boundaries between clauses and phrases within the sentence, allowing the writer to combine different elements in longer sentences.

Independent activities

Children complete questions A and B in the pupils' book. Offer PCM 24B to early finishers. This is an investigation using another extract from *Alice's Adventures in Wonderland*. Punctuation marks have been swapped for numbers; pupils complete a key to indicate which is which. This activity may work best in pairs or could be offered as homework.

Plenary

Consider the impact of changing punctuation marks on sentences. Have pupils achieved any bizarre or amusing effects, for example by swapping exclamation marks with question marks, changing full stops and moving apostrophes?

Session 3

You will need pupils' book 3, Unit 24, pages 54–5, and the Reminder Sheet.

Shared writing

1 You will be writing about an incident in which a child experiences a magical change.

2 Begin by working on the character and setting. Discuss elements of the character's age/gender/ appearance/personality, and the setting: past, present or future; the place; objects.

3 Consider the changing event. The character could drink, eat or smell something; use a key to open a door etc.

4 Finally, discuss what will happen to the character. It may be a physical change, or a change in some aspect of personality.

5 Explain that you will be using some elements of Carroll's style. You have already set up a similar situation; what language features will be necessary? Consider sentence length, use of punctuation, the way the characters talk to themselves, etc.

Write together

1 Begin by composing the first sentence, in which the character finds the potion etc. Use the first sentence from the OHT or pupils' book extract as a model, e.g.
Eventually, James found himself in a bathroom with a basin and, as he had expected, a toothbrush and toothpaste: he picked up the toothpaste and was just about to brush his teeth when he noticed a label on the side of the tube.

2 Work on this sentence, checking that it contains the correct elements. Can it be extended at all? Should it be? Check that punctuation is accurate.

Independent writing activity

Pupils continue writing the story. They may use the text in the pupils' book as a guide, or for ideas. Offer other work by Carroll for reference.

Work with groups of pupils who find this activity challenging, encouraging them to use original sentences as models for their own writing. Look particularly at the way in which these move the story along.

Plenary

Share pieces of writing of which pupils are proud. Ask them to describe how they went about imitating Carroll's style, and what they found difficult about it. Ask all pupils to look for the longest sentence they have written, and check these make sense. Pupils continue writing for homework, until they have completed a section.

Session 4

You will need a section of work you have written, or one written by a pupil, on OHT, and the Reminder Sheet.

Shared writing

Explain that you will be editing and revising work.

Write together

Display the text on which you will be working, and read it aloud. Thinking aloud, look at places where the meaning is unclear, or ideas could be developed. Mark these with brief notes in the margin. Demonstrate how a writer might tackle these problems. Take contributions, and demonstrate the use of editing marks. Make sure punctuation is accurate.

Independent writing activity

Pupils exchange work with a partner. Allow ten minutes for them to read the piece they have received and to edit it, making suggestions as demonstrated. They then revise their edited pieces.

Plenary

Discuss revisions. Do pupils feel the revised piece is improved? Discuss a possible format for publication.

Assessment

Pupils should be able to:
• use longer sentences
• punctuate sentences accurately
• describe the function of different punctuation marks in complex sentences.

Provide additional support to pupils who find manipulation of longer sentences difficult. Ask pupils to evaluate how similar their work is to Carroll's, and how they have achieved the effect.

Model answers

Pupils' book 3 ☐ A

1 Because they were attractive.
2 Answers may vary: simple curiosity, or boredom (although this seems unlikely!). Most pupils will think she was not wise.
3 Pupils may suggest that it would have had a name for the liquid, a list of ingredients, or a warning.
4 She cannot get out, and may be crushed.
5 Answers will vary: find an antidote, break the house.

Pupils' book 3 ☐ B

6 The first sentence is the longest. Make sure pupils list all the punctuation marks and reasons for them.
7 Answers will vary.

24A   Punctuating longer sentences ▣
Answers will vary. Focus on how easy sentences are to understand and how well they read rather than sentence length alone.

24B   Replacing punctuation ▣
1 Full stop .
2 Inverted comma '
3 Colon :
4 Exclamation mark !
5 Apostrophe '
6 Inverted comma '
7 Semi-colon ;
8 Comma ,
9 Question mark ?

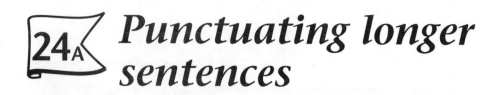

24A Punctuating longer sentences

Longer and longer!

Here are some short sentences. Combine them to make longer sentences, building up to one sentence. Remember to use punctuation carefully:

, (comma)   ; (semi-colon)   : (colon)   – (dash)

Sentences	Text
5	Haddiyah sat on a chair. She was thinking about her mother. Her mother was going for a job interview. Haddiyah wasn't sure that she wanted her mother to get the job. She might have to stay away from home sometimes.
3	
1	

If you finish, try to extend the sentence even further. There are 40 words in the five sentences – that's eight words per sentence. How close can you get to Carroll's 109?

_____

_____

_____

_____

24B Replacing punctuation

More magic

In this excerpt, the punctuation marks have been replaced by numbers. Read through the whole piece, then try to work out which number represents which punctuation mark, and complete the key at the bottom.

As she said this she looked down at her hands$_8$ and was surprised to see that she had put on one of the Rabbits$_5$ little white kid gloves while she was talking$_1$ $_2$How can I have done that$_9$$_6$ she thought$_8$ $_2$I must be growing small again$_1$$_6$ She got up and went to the table to measure herself by it$_8$ and found that$_8$ as nearly as she could guess$_8$ she was now about two feet high$_8$ and was going on shrinking rapidly$_3$ she soon found out that the cause of this was the fan she was holding$_8$ and she dropped it hastily$_8$ just in time to save herself from shrinking away altogether$_1$

$_2$That was a narrow escape$_4$$_6$ said Alice$_8$ a good deal frightened at the sudden change$_8$ but very glad to find herself still in existence$_7$ $_2$and now for the garden$_4$$_6$ and she ran with all speed back to the little door$_3$ but$_8$ alas$_4$ the little door was shut again$_8$ and the little golden key was lying on the glass table as before$_8$ $_2$and things are worse than ever$_8$$_6$ thought the poor child$_8$ $_2$for I never was so small as this before$_8$ never$_4$ And I declare it's$_5$ too bad$_8$ that it is$_4$$_6$

As she said these words her foot slipped$_8$ and in another moment$_8$ splash$_4$ she was up to her chin in salt water$_1$

From Alice's Adventures in Wonderland by Lewis Carroll

Apostrophe	Colon	Comma	Exclamation mark	Full stop	Inverted comma	Inverted comma	Question mark	Semi-colon
'	:	,	!	.	'	'	?	;

24 Punctuating complex sentences

When you are using complex sentences in your writing, it is important to make sure that you punctuate them carefully, otherwise readers will have great difficulty reading them.

. ? !	Start every sentence with a capital letter and end it with a full stop / question mark / exclamation mark.
,	Use commas to separate clauses and phrases from the rest of the sentence. You can also sometimes use them instead of brackets.
:	Use colons to introduce lists, and to add detail to a sentence.
;	Use a semi-colon to separate items in a list, especially where each item has more than one word. You can also use them to link sentences.
( ) –	Use brackets or dashes to put in extra information that is not essential to the text. For example: *Alice – the little girl in the story – drank the potion.*

Using apostrophes

The purpose of this unit is for pupils to revise and extend their understanding and accurate use of possessive apostrophes.

NLS coverage

Key objective
SL 5 To revise the use of apostrophes for possession

Learned through
TL **Reading comprehension and writing composition**
2 To identify the point of view from which a story is told and how this affects the reader's response
7 To write from another character's point of view, e.g. retelling an incident in letter form

Assessment criteria
SL By the end of this unit, pupils should be able to identify the use of the apostrophe, i.e. for contraction/possession; explain rules for use of the apostrophe in possessives; use apostrophes accurately in independent writing.

TL **Reading comprehension and writing composition**
Children should be able to identify the point of view from which a story is told and retell an incident from a different point of view.

Session 1

You will need OHT 25 and PCM 25A.

Shared reading

1 Introduce the OHT text – about a child going to a new school. Have any pupils ever changed school? Invite those who have to talk about how they felt on their first sight of their new school. Explain that pupils should try to find out as much as they can about the main character from what they read.

2 Display and read OHT 25. Ask pupils what they have learned about the main character. Discuss physical appearance and personality. What do pupils feel about gender? Are there any clues in the story?

3 What else can pupils divine about the character? Discuss previous experience and expectations of this individual.

4 Consider how the girl in the playground might see the main character, and the scene at the school. Compare the two different points of view.

Sentence level work

1 Discuss the punctuation marks in this story. There are lots of different ones, but one in particular that is frequently used incorrectly – the apostrophe.

2 Ask pupils to explain what they know about apostrophes. They should be able to give two reasons for using an apostrophe – in contracted words such as *I've*, and to denote the possessive (*'s* and *s'*).

3 There are many theories about why apostrophes are used in this way. For example, William Shakespeare sometimes uses *es* for possessives. If this was common, then the apostrophe for possession could actually be showing where a letter *e* has been omitted. This is only one theory of many!

4 Make sure pupils know when they should <u>not</u> use an apostrophe. (In a plural!)
Discuss where – if anywhere – apostrophes should be placed in the following sentences:

Susans dogs are Labradors.
I love reading books.
I hate peoples alarms going off in the night.

Independent activities

Pupils should complete PCM 25A, which contains many apostrophes – not all correctly placed! PCM 25B is an alternative activity, using the same text, in which there are no apostrophes at all.

Plenary

Ask pupils to look at how they have corrected the texts: which were the most difficult items to solve?

Session 2

You will need pupils' book 3, Unit 25, pages 56–7.

Shared reading

1 Explain that you will be reading an excerpt from the first Harry Potter novel. Ask pupils who have read the book, from whose point of view they think the incident will be told.

2 Ask pupils to turn to the pupils' book. Read the text aloud while the children follow. Allow pupils to reread the text – were they right about the point of view from which it is told?

3 Encourage pupils to discuss how Ron, Hermione and the troll itself may have been feeling during the incident. Look for evidence in the text.

Sentence level work

1 Remind pupils of the two functions of apostrophes. Talk further about the apostrophe. Previously, punctuation has been discussed as something that helps the reader. Does the apostrophe help the reader get to the meaning of the text? Does it have any impact on expressive reading?

2 Why is so much time devoted to the apostrophe? It is really quite simple, but it causes so much confusion! Allow pupils to look back at the last three pieces they have written, and see how accurate their use of apostrophes has been. Has anyone not made any errors? Set a target for the class – how accurate do they think it is possible to be?

Independent activities

Children complete A and B in the pupils' book.

Plenary

Compare notes – did pupils identify apostrophes accurately? Discuss this.

Session 3

You will need pupils' book 3, Unit 25, pages 56–7, and the Reminder Sheet.

Shared writing

Explain that you will be writing up the incident from another point of view. Begin by listing the events which happen, and what is known about the setting and people involved. List these on the board. Select either Ron's or Hermione's point of view to use.

Write together
Begin writing with the pupils. Remind them about use of the first person. Emphasize the differences between the viewpoints of the characters, and their interpretations of the action. Discuss the use of apostrophes when they come up, reminding pupils of the class focus on accurate apostrophes.

Independent writing activity

Direct pupils to:
- complete the piece you have started with them, altering as necessary, or
- write from the other child's point of view.

Support pupils as necessary.

Plenary

Discuss how pupils felt about the character from whose viewpoint they were writing.

Session 4

You will need pupils' book 3, Unit 25, pages 56–7, and the Reminder Sheet.

Shared writing

A more challenging task: to write about the same incident from the point of view of the fourth character involved in the incident – the troll! Refer back to the outline of the incident from the previous session. Explain that this piece will begin slightly before Ron and Harry hear Hermione scream.

Write together
Write the first paragraph together. Focus on how the troll would have been feeling – the mixture of emotions.

Independent writing activity

Pupils should continue writing. Some may adopt the opening sentence that was written together; others may choose to start from scratch.

Plenary

Ask pupils to reflect on their writing, and go back to their use of apostrophes. How easy did they find it to write and punctuate at the same time? Discuss strategies: some will find that they focus on punctuation more at the editing stage; others will feel comfortable with punctuation, so that it becomes second nature. Either is acceptable – everyone has different strategies. Discuss ways of coping with individual style.

Assessment

Pupils should be able to:
- use apostrophes accurately
- differentiate between characters' responses and emotions
- retell an incident in a story from a different point of view.

Model answers

Pupils' book 3 ◹ A

1 The word *victory* suggests they had just had a fight.
2 Pupils may suggest: strong but clumsy (it broke the sinks), and refer to Rowling's choice of vocabulary (*lumbered, blinking stupidly; mean little eyes; ugly snout*). It also seems aggressive (because of its behaviour).
3 She was too frightened to do anything at all.
4 Answers will vary, but should be justified.

Pupils' book 3 ◹ B

5

Possession	Omission
girls'	they'd
troll's	It's
Harry's	didn't
troll's	couldn't

6 Check that pupils have used apostrophes correctly.

◹ 25A   Correcting apostrophes ▣

Apostrophes to delete: others (line 1); games (line 2); boys (line 5); pens (line 9); asks (line 16)
Apostrophes to add: that's (line 15); John's (line 18)

◹ 25B   Putting in the apostrophes ▣

Apostrophes to add: I'd (line 6); boy's (line 10); wasn't (line 13); who'd (line 13); that's (line 15); I've (line 17); I'll (line 17); John's (line 18)

Correcting apostrophes

There are many apostrophes in this story. Check them and delete any that are incorrect. The writer may also have missed some – add these in.

The New Kid

The bell went, and all the others' stopped playing their game's and lined up in the yard. Where should I go? The headteacher saw me – I must have stuck out like a sore thumb – and called me over. She told me which class to go into, and called one of the boys' over to show me where to go.

As I walked into the class, I realized that the girl I'd seen in the playground was sitting with her mates. I went and sat with some other boys, and took off my coat. I had nothing in my bag – not even any pens'. The teacher was OK about it, though. I borrowed one boy's pencil and ruler, and started to work.

All morning I was dreading playtime, but when it came, it wasn't so bad. Scott – the boy who'd lent me his stuff – asked me if I wanted to join in with their football game, and so thats what I did.

There will come a time, though, when someone asks' me where I've come from, and why I changed schools. I'll ask Johns opinion, but I know it will be my decision what I tell them.

Putting in the apostrophes

The writer of this text had a faulty apostrophe key on his computer! Can you place the apostrophes correctly?

The New Kid

The bell went, and all the others stopped playing their games and lined up in the yard. Where should I go? The headteacher saw me – I must have stuck out like a sore thumb – and called me over. She told me which class to go into, and called one of the boys over to show me where to go.

As I walked into the class, I realized that the girl Id seen in the playground was sitting with her mates. I went and sat with some other boys, and took off my coat. I had nothing in my bag – not even any pens. The teacher was OK about it, though. I borrowed one boys pencil and ruler, and started to work.

All morning I was dreading playtime, but when it came, it wasnt so bad. Scott – the boy whod lent me his stuff – asked me if I wanted to join in with their football game, and so thats what I did.

There will come a time, though, when someone asks me where Ive come from, and why I changed schools. Ill ask Johns opinion, but I know it will be my decision what I tell them.

25 | *Using apostrophes*

This punctuation mark causes more problems than any other! It has two main uses:

Missing letters

When two or more words are contracted to make a shorter word, an apostrophe is used to show where letters have been dropped.
For example:

> *does + not = doesn't*
> *could + have = could've*

Possession

An apostrophe can be used to show ownership.

- Where there is only one owner, the apostrophe comes <u>before</u> the s.
  For example:
  The cat's whiskers are long.
  That is Sunita's book.

- If an item has more than one owner, the apostrophe comes <u>after</u> the s.
  For example:
  This is my parents' room.
  Where is the boys' father?

- If there is a singular noun representing a group (e.g. *children, people*), this is treated as a single owner.
  For example:
  I have lost the children's gloves.
  Lions were the people's choice.

Remember

Be careful with *its*.
The apostrophe is used to mark contraction (*it + is = it's*),
but not possession *(Where is its owner?)*